JOURNEY IN GRACE

ONE WOMAN'S PROGRESSIVE REVELATION OF THE GRACE OF GOD

BY GLORIA HARTMAN

PRESS

I hope this
pleases you.

Gloria Hartman
9/2/05

<u>This book is dedicated to:</u>

The memory of my husband for 39 ½ years

Gerald William Hartman
Who moved to heaven
On February 25, 1999

ACKNOWLEDGEMENTS

I would like to take this public avenue to express my sincere love and appreciation to my children: Mark William Hartman and Deborah Darlene Todd. During the most difficult time of my life, they loved me enough to give me my freedom to find my way with Jesus and, at the same time, be there for me whenever I have needed them. They have truly, "taken care of Mama."

I would also like to thank my sister and brother-in-law, Linda & Fred Thompson, for opening their home to me, in the community in which I needed to live, to get myself settled and to write this book. I am forever grateful.

TABLE OF CONTENTS

INTRODUCTION

My life has truly been a progressive revelation of the grace of God. My earliest recollections of hearing about the Lord were of hearing preaching from the Bible and being encouraged to believe what He had said in His Word. As a child, I knew very little, but I was fortunate enough to have been raised under the influence of preaching which stressed salvation by grace through faith.

As I went along in my life, I was led into many deeper revelations of the grace of God. My husband was responsible for seeking further into the things of God, and for leading me along with him. I will always be grateful.

As I have written this book, it has been my desire to tell you my story and, with the telling, share with you the truths I have learned about God and about me. I am a teacher but the way the Lord uses me to convey truth from His Word is to teach, in a practical way, from what I have learned myself. Therefore, this is not so much a book teaching about the doctrine of grace but a telling of a story, with some teaching thrown in.

I have poured out my heart as I have told my story. A few of these chapters were written through my tears. I hope you enjoy what I have written. But – more than that, I trust that you will be helped, as you read about me and what I have learned about God and me.

Gloria Hartman

CHAPTER ONE

WHY I WAS THE WAY I WAS

I was raised in a mid-western city by parents who had both been raised in a rural community and, therefore, had the work ethic, religious background, and moral attitudes common to the mid-west. I have heard us described as "salt of the earth" kind of people – people who work hard; people who are honest; people who go to church; and people who are slow to trust people from the eastern or western coasts. I was raised in a denominational church and heard the Gospel often as a child. At 13, I accepted Christ as my Personal Savior and was baptized in water. I have to say, though, that my moral attitudes through my teen years were more a result of my upbringing than any notable change in my life as a result of inviting Jesus into my life. The emphasis of which I was aware in my church-going was on being saved from Hell. There were things in the world which one wasn't supposed to do, as a church-goer, but those were the same things of which I had been made aware in my upbringing. I don't ever recall being taught that Jesus in me would change me on the inside. There only seemed to be an emphasis on what I did – my actions, or lifestyle.

I do remember sitting in church when there would be a visiting missionary speaking about a life dedicated to Christ. Primarily it was rededication, and, as I understood it, directed at someone who had gotten away from the Lord and was returning, or someone who was dedicating his or her life to the mission field. As a girl, the mission field seemed the only option open to me; so, even though I felt "compelled" to do that, the mission field seemed very extreme to me and not where I wanted to go. Therefore, I remember thinking deep somewhere in me, "Someday when I'm old, maybe there'll be somewhere to go and do something for God – but not now." I now know that there was a call on my life. Through lack of teaching, I did not recognize it as such and, therefore, ignored it.

I had a severely "crossed eye" as a youngster and wore glasses from 3 years of age on. I developed an extreme inferiority complex in the social realm of life. My family was very loving and I had no problems there. I was an above average student – no big problems there. Socially, I felt like a failure. I did not feel "beautiful" and constantly was aware of the way I looked and felt that I didn't measure up. I decided, in my second year of college, to have two eye surgeries (which it would take to solve my problem) as soon as the second semester was over. I knew I would have to pay for it myself. My parents couldn't afford it and, since it was considered "cosmetic" surgery, it was not covered in any type of insurance we had. I searched and found an eye surgeon which would do the surgery and let me pay for it after I had recuperated, found a job and could begin to make payments to him. I left college at the end of the second year. I could not afford to go on. I had the two eye surgeries and after the healing, for the first time in my life, I felt "beautiful." I got a secretarial job and began to pay the eye doctor. I lived at home with my family. I was so entranced with the way I looked now that, often, I would go without my glasses. I couldn't see well at all. The surgery did not help my vision, which was very bad in the eye which had been crossed, and a little bit bad in my good eye. It only made me look "normal." Of course, I wore my glasses when I was working but I took them off much of the rest of the time. I tried to be very careful about where I was going so I wouldn't have an accident. I knew I couldn't see well. Ah – vanity!

My social life did not change drastically because I was not a real out-going person but the way I felt about myself changed. I liked me now. For the next year, I lived, by the normal standards of the '50's, a very boring lifestyle; but to me, it was fun and exciting. I worked, paid my bills, dressed nicely, went out with both female and male friends and, for the most part, enjoyed life. I knew I was a Christian but I was pretty much the kind of Christian who prays desperately in a pinch, or a rough time, and forgets about it most of the rest of the time. I remember thinking one day, as I sat in church, "It seems like they are talking, when they pray here in church, to 'Someone' different than the One that I talk to. I just talk – like I do to a friend. They talk so religious and holy. I wonder if I'm wrong to talk to God like I do." Sometimes I would get prayers answered. Not often, though!! I had no idea why sometimes it would work and most of the time it did not.

THEN – One Day I Fell in Love!!! I met a man on a blind date arranged by a friend of mine. I had been recently disillusioned by the lifestyle of the man that I had been seeing and had broken up with him. I was not anxious, at that time, to meet someone else. Not wanting to hurt my friend's feelings, I agreed to the date. We met. It was, what the world calls, "love at first sight." We never dated anyone else. He treated me like a queen. He was romantic. He was handsome. He was 2 years older than me and we were both in our early 20's. He was in the military service and was expecting to get his orders for overseas duty shortly. It was after the Korean War so we were not afraid of active battle, but things were very strained on the world scene, and we were young and in love. He proposed on our second date, which was the next day after the first date. I didn't accept until the third date, which was the next day after the second date. We decided that it would only be between us, though, for awhile. I knew that my parents would have a difficult time with it being so quick. I was very close to my family, especially my father, and I couldn't stand the thought of disappointing him.

Two weeks later, we started to "go steady," (in the '50's this meant that I wore his ring on a chain around my neck). Three weeks after that, he gave me a diamond engagement ring, and we were formally engaged. The next month and one-half was a whirlwind time because he got his orders and he was going to Korea for 13 months. We decided to not get married until he returned. This was a very hard decision to make. I felt that a "hurry-up" wedding would be a big problem to my parents and we decided to honor them by not putting them through that. We decided that we had waited all our lives for one another and that we could wait "for each other" a little while longer. We decided, at that point, that we would never be apart from one another after we were married – that all we needed was each other.

He shipped out to Korea and I began to plan a wedding. Thirteen months later, he returned to our city on a Monday and a fairly large church wedding was planned for the following Friday. I had everything organized – down to the smallest detail. It was a lovely "50's" wedding. I had a beautiful white dress, which I wore with "honor." Everything was perfect. My new husband, being the romantic that he was, picked up my bags in the afternoon (our wedding was planned for that evening) and took them to our hotel. Of course, according to tradition, which my grandmother and my mother saw to, we were not allowed to see each other until the wedding. As he took our bags to our hotel room, he made sure that everything was perfect. Is it any wonder that I had stars in my eyes!!

As I reflect, I realize that it was at that time that *MY MARRIAGE BEGAN TO TAKE FIRST PLACE IN MY LIFE.* Of course, I didn't realize it then. However, as I look back, nothing – absolutely nothing – was more important to me than my marriage. I knew that my husband wasn't perfect. I knew that he had little flaws in his personality and imperfections in his habit patterns. If I didn't know about them before the wedding, I certainly discovered his moods, his little irritating habits, etc. as we began to live together. It was not hard for me to forgive those things though because he was my "Knight in Shining Armor."

Exactly one month after we got married, we were at the home of the man (and his wife) who was my husband's best man at our wedding. We had been invited to their home for dinner. After dinner, my husband's friend took him into another room and they stayed in there for a long time. I was extremely uncomfortable. I had been assessing that this couple seemed very "religious." (I found out later that, during the time my husband had been in Korea, this couple had become Christians.) The two men came back to where we were about 2 ½ hours later and we prepared to go. I was so anxious to get out of there and find out what was going on. I resented the way the evening had gone. As we left, my husband's friend said to me, "He has something to tell you when you get to the car." He sounded so excited and was all "smiley."

When we got in the car, my husband told me that he had become a Christian – that he was "saved" – that he had accepted Jesus into his life. I was stunned. This was something that was supposed to happen in church. Besides that, he had grown up in the same denomination that I had (at least much of his life) and I had assumed that he was a Christian. When we had met with my pastor before we were married, there had been no problem. My pastor had not quizzed him about this. I felt that this was a personal matter that these people had no right in butting into.

In that 2 ½ hour period, "Something" had come between us. It seemed that things were different now. He didn't need just me. He was bringing God into this. I didn't like it. Over the next several months, I felt like he was dragging me to one Bible study after another. These were Bible studies in people's homes. We also started attending the same church that the "couple" attended. It was a non-denominational church and everyone carried a Bible and a notebook. They wrote in their Bibles. They acted like they were all students and seemed to write constantly during church. Also, the sermon seemed to last forever. I was very reserved and really didn't feel like I fit. They gave testimonies once a month on Sunday evenings and scheduled my husband to do that. This was a "stand at the pulpit and talk from notes" kind of testimony and I was a nervous wreck. He was to be water baptized the same night.

I felt like our "fairy-tale romance" was being messed up. I was miserable. I didn't feel like I had a "testimony." In fact, I was seriously in doubt as to whether I was even a Christian. After weeks of this misery, one night when I was alone in our apartment, I knelt by my bed and prayed this prayer, "Lord, I don't know whether I am a Christian or not. My husband has become a Christian and has really changed. He loves You now, I think, more than me. He wants to read the Bible now; he wants to go to church all the time and Bible studies all the time. I feel like everything is all fouled up. So – I'm asking You to do for me what You did for him. If I am already saved, do in me what You did in Him. If I'm not saved, then I want to be right now. I want us to be together in this. I don't want anything between us. I do love You. But this whole way of thinking is all new to me, just when I was getting used to being married. Jesus, I thought You were already in me, but if You're not, then please come into me right now. I have learned that the Bible says that if we ask, You will do it. So, I believe I am a Christian. I am saved."

My motivation for praying that prayer was to be together with my husband, because you see, my marriage really had first place in my life. I was "head over heels" in love with my husband. I don't mean that I agreed with him about everything. I knew he wasn't the smartest man in the world. He wasn't the handsomest man in the world, and he sure didn't make a lot of money. But – he treated me so special. He told me constantly how much he loved me and how pretty I was.

After praying that prayer, I had my first real lesson in faith. I learned that I had to put into practical living what I had prayed. If I truly believed in God, and that He heard and answered prayer, then I had to believe that He had heard me when I prayed and that He had done what I asked. I didn't feel any different, but I just began to act as though God had done it. I prayed with my husband, memorized scripture verses with my husband, went to Bible studies with him, and talked to the Lord as though He knew me personally and was interested in every detail of my life. I now know that I was putting action to my faith, and that I was "putting on the new man." After awhile, it was not an effort. It began to come naturally to me to live as a Christian. I began to read and study the Bible with fervor. I discovered that the Lord would give me insight into His Word. My zealousness to read and study the Word of God and to grow as a Christian had a weight dragging it down much of the time, though. By this time, I had discovered that my husband, who had embraced the Christian life with such vigor, also had some problems. He seemed to be what I have termed a "yo-yo Christian." I now know that these problems which he encountered much of the time were nothing but "works of the flesh." He tended to want to go back to his old life, before he was a Christian, and grab hold of old habits, old ways of talking, old ways of thinking. Then, after awhile, he would be so upset with himself. He would pray, repent, feel bad, get all straightened out with the Lord – and we would go on.

As I look back on it now, I can see that I developed a habit pattern in dealing with it. My husband was a very strong personality and very persuasive. I didn't want to argue with him. By this time, I had heard about "submission," and I certainly didn't want to be considered a wife who did not submit to her husband. When he would go through these frequent lifestyle changes, I would resist at first. Then I would become very confused about what my role and attitude was to be. I loved him so dearly and I knew he loved me. Eventually, he would win out and I would follow him in his lifestyle away from the "sold out" Christian life. Then, when he got to feeling so bad, and wanted to make a change back to the things of God, I would come back with him. What a way to live! You see, my marriage was so important to me that I couldn't bear the thought of us being divided on anything. So I followed him.

When we celebrated our second anniversary, we were about to have our second child. We had a boy and a girl, who were born eleven months apart. We kept trying to live for God but we honestly just didn't know how. My husband battled with his on-again, off-again Christianity and I followed him because I loved him. We were a new family in the early 60's and we never seemed to have enough money. My husband changed jobs frequently. He did not have a college education but seemed to be able to do several kinds of things quite well. He was always trying to find just the right thing. I had done executive secretarial work so before, between, and after babies I worked here and there to bring in extra money. He was always just a little bit amazed at my ability to always find a decent paying job and always praised me. I think there was a bit of jealousy perhaps but he would have denied it had I brought it up, which I never would have done. I really did not ever want to do anything to put him down, to cause him to feel bad about himself, or anything in that realm. That is not because I was so spiritual. It is because I didn't want to risk him getting depressed because things were not going as he thought they would and his taking another little trip "into the world." I definitely did not like "yo-yo Christianity," but I did not know how to change it.

CHAPTER TWO

WHITHER THOU GOEST, I WILL GO

When our children were about 5 and 6 years of age, we went through a spiritual "awakening," which I truly thought was the answer to our dilemmas in life. We had spent a considerable amount of time just soaking in the Word of God. We seemed to be just unable to get enough of the Word, of teaching, of music, of all things connected with God. The deeper we got into the Word of God, and the more understanding we seemed to get, the more we began to feel that we should go to Bible School and prepare for the ministry. When you are the only one in your family, in your workplace, etc. who is very, very involved in the study of the Word of God, you begin to take to heart what everyone says about you. You begin to wonder if you really should go into the ministry. You hear all kinds of things about the "call." We honestly didn't know if we were or not. I was sure that I wasn't. If there was such a thing as a "call," it had to be on the man, I thought, because God didn't use women in the ministry – that is, unless they went to the mission field somewhere. I really didn't question that. I just accepted it. As I reflect, I really believe that my husband thought that God had been bringing him all along the way in his life to this point. He had never found the right "niche" in a career, and, to be really honest about it, he had never really wanted to study anything before in his life.

Wanting to "study," the Bible was a first. He was worried about the ability to study after being out of high school so many years but he believed that God would help him. I had honestly begun to believe that, as we pursued Bible School and whatever field of ministry God led us into, we would find the peace and contentment that had seemed to always be just out of our reach. I figured that, as we began to follow "God's plan for our lives," things would even out for us and my husband would be content, growing in the Lord and in the things of God. I thought that the "pull" toward the world when things weren't going right would wane as we were absorbed in the things of God.

We so wanted to serve God with our lives. We wanted to be in the center of His will. We knew just about a thimble full about faith. We read books about great men of faith and we read and studied the Word. We began to look into Bible Schools and found a non-denominational, fundamental Bible School in Canada that seemed to be cheaper to attend than most of the others. It was a long way from the Midwest for a family of four to go, "by faith." But go we did.

We spent one year in Canada and then transferred to a Bible School in Colorado. Those years of Bible School were some of the worst and some of the best of our lives. There were so many money problems and so many problems with my husband trying to learn how to study really for the first time in his life. We had the normal problems of two young children beginning school and with the added stress of being completely away from their grandparents, to whom they had become very close in their young lives. The very worst part of those years was neither of us understood how to live the Christian life, as we could read in the Word that it was supposed to be lived. It seemed so impossible. The only way we seemed to be able to get by was to live our private lives with all of our very personal doubts, fears, problems, etc., and then to live our public lives like it seemed everyone else lived – as though we were on top of everything. I have sense learned that a very large percentage of Christians live that way every day of their lives.

I said that they were also some of the best years of our lives. That is because we learned that, in spite of our troubles, our confusion, our doubts, our tempers, our mistakes, etc., God met our needs over and over again even though we didn't know what we were doing. We didn't have much in the way of material things through those years but we always had a place to live and, even though we went for a period of time in Canada with not much else to eat but potatoes, we still always managed to feed our children. The "potato times," as we fondly remembered them in later years were very scary and hard to endure. We had 100 pound bags of potatoes given to us and not much else. The money was gone. We had utilized every potato recipe I could get my hands on. Then we began to run out of all the other things that were needed with potatoes to make various dishes – 'til there were only potatoes left. Even the tea, coffee, and powdered milk were gone. We were about to despair. We had felt very strongly that we should not tell people that we had a need. We were so embarrassed. We didn't let our families know what we were going through.

One morning, in my devotions, I was reading in Psalm 37. I came to verse 25. "I have been young, and now am old; yet have I not seen the righteous forsaken, nor his seed begging bread." It seemed to jump off the page at me. I was crying as I read, but then I really began to sob. I prayed something like this, "Lord, David said this but the New Testament says that I am righteous because of Jesus Christ. He is my Savior and Lord. David said that he had never seen the righteous forsaken and that he had never seen the seed of the righteous have to beg for bread. Lord, we need food. My children need food. If You took care of them then, in the Old Testament, You can take care of us now. Jesus said in the New Testament that if we asked in His name, You would do it. I'm asking in His name – the name of Jesus. Please bring food to us."

I went about the morning and afternoon. We had potatoes – boiled I believe – for lunch and dinner with water to drink. It was absolutely awful. We put the children to bed. After they had been in bed for about 30 minutes, there was a knock at our door. My husband went to the door and one of my husband's Bible teachers, a former missionary to China, was at our door with two or three people. They had several large boxes of groceries and began carrying them into our house. They covered a large area with all of this food, and just as quickly as they came, they left. My husband and I were in shock. We could hardly believe our eyes. There was every kind of food imaginable, with fresh milk, vegetables, and meat. There were even bags of cookies. I cannot begin to explain to you the magnificent joy we were feeling. We got the children back up and brought them in to see all that food. They just stared with open mouths. We poured milk for everybody and ate cookies and milk. We truly had a party. Our God was faithful!

We had many miracles of provision during those years. One time, we were awakened in the middle of the night with a strange noise on the floor of our tiny, ground floor apartment. We always locked our door and had never been worried about someone trying to get in. My husband stumbled over something in the living room, trying to get to the door. As he got to the door and opened it, it was still locked, but there was a large, black limousine driving away. The Bible School was located in a rural community in Canada and we were living on campus. This was not a common sight. Stunned, he closed the door again and turned to turn on the light, just as I got in the living room after getting into my robe. Our eyes both fell on two very large boxes of groceries in the middle of the floor, containing lots and lots of food. We never knew who delivered those groceries in that big, black limousine. We never knew how that locked door was opened and then locked again. My husband always believed that it was an angel. We couldn't prove it, of course, but nobody could prove that it wasn't. We never saw that limousine again, and nobody ever said anything to us which sounded like human involvement.

We somehow managed to get by during those years, with our school bills paid and our children fed, clothed, and provided for in all the ways that matter. We had begun to believe that we would probably apply to a mission organization and think about going overseas. We seemed to have an interest in working with American servicemen and were seriously considering Christian Servicemen's Center work in one of the countries where there are American bases. However, as my husband got to his last year of Bible School, we became aware of the need for pastors to pastor small churches just getting going in the mountains of Colorado. One in particular was of interest to us and, within a few short weeks, we found ourselves moving to the mountains to pastor a small, community church. The Lord provided housing for us rent free and utilities provided. He had been doing things like that for us all the way through Bible School.

We had lived for one summer, rent free, utilities provided in a huge mansion, which, by today's standards, would be worth several million dollars. All we had to do was just be there. Another time we lived in the foothills with a gorgeous view, for a very small amount of money. Another time, we lived in a lovely suburban home for about ¼ of what it could have rented for. Of course, we moved several times. It almost became a way of life. My husband and I both worked at various jobs while he got his degree in Biblical Education.

This new home in the mountains was a breathtakingly beautiful location. We were embarking on a whole new adventure – actually pastoring a church. It wasn't much of a church, but we felt like God had opened doors for us and was leading us into His perfect will. During that first year of pastoring, my husband graduated from Bible School and was also ordained to the ministry. My husband felt like he had finally accomplished something worthwhile in his life. Bible School had been difficult for him. I typed so many term papers, corrected spelling, grammar, punctuation, etc. that I felt that my name ought to be on that degree also. Of course, I never said that to him. I praised him and was very vocal in letting him know how proud I was of his accomplishment. When he was ordained, I truly never gave it a thought about him being ordained and not me. In the circles of Christendom with which we were familiar, women were not ordained Women were never on the platform of a church, except to sing, or to give a special announcement regarding a specific thing. Of course, when a missionary couple would visit, the woman was expected to say a little something but not too much.

I saw being a pastor's wife as just another extension of my role in life anyway, which was to be everything I could be to my husband. With him being a pastor, we could be together almost all the time. Remember, my marriage to my man was all important to me. My relationship with the Lord was tied to my relationship with my husband. When my husband made mistakes or had problems of one sort or another, I truly never got so mad at him that I threatened to leave him. If I was really upset with him, I portrayed it to him as hurt in me – never anger at him. I saw our relationship like this. What he was strong in, I was weak in; and what he was weak in, I was strong in. I saw the two of us coming together and making a strong single unit. I figured that my strengths could always make up for his weaknesses and his strengths could always make up for my weaknesses. Therefore, in my mind, together, we were unbeatable doing the Lord's work. I knew that there were some things in the life of a pastor that he might have trouble with, but I would help him through those. Together we could do the job. He was strong and bold. I had the social graces and was strong with words. He depended on me and I depended on him. I did not think of myself as a unique individual all by myself. I thought about myself as my husband's wife. My role in life was to be supportive to him. Remember – my relationship with God was all connected with my relationship with my husband. He was not dictatorial or demanding with me and, for the most part, we related to each other in most matters very well.

CHAPTER THREE

POWER IN MY LIFE?

We entered into the pastorate of that first church with great gusto. We found it to be fun. We loved being able to talk about the things of God for a living. We loved visiting with people and leading them into a deeper relationship with the Lord. After that first year, another community church in the mountains was in need of a pastor and, through the normal channels observed in that area, my husband preached at the church and was examined by the Board. We were asked to come and pastor that church. It was quite a step up because this church had a lovely parsonage, next-door to the church. What more could we want? We had a beautiful place to live and minister in and a great place for our kids.

There was a gnawing uneasiness in me many times that we did not find the Christian life any easier to live than we had before we went to Bible School. We had a great deal of Bible knowledge and were very familiar with the great doctrines of the church but when it came right down to daily living for Jesus, it was well nigh impossible it seemed. Over the years, we had pretty much established a lifestyle pattern of private living and public living. There were ways of thinking in us which were contrary to the Word, but we didn't even think about them anymore. We just kept that in our private life and away from public view.

We were self-deceived but we didn't know it. Because of that, we did not make many really close friends. We had lots and lots of acquaintances and most of the people in our churches considered us open with them but, as I look back, we never let most of them get too close. They might see something in us that we felt had to stay hidden. We never discussed this. It was just understood between us. We were very close to each other. We knew how each other felt on just about everything and we always tried to do the thing that would make the other one look good.

In those first few years of pastoring those small mountain churches, it seemed to be understood that the pastor's wife was to lead Bible studies for the women of the church. Before we had moved to the mountains, I had been involved in a city-wide, non-denominational women's group where we had groups of about 20 to 30 for Bible discussions. There was a leader for each of the groups. I was one of those leaders and we would meet, in our own individual groups on a certain day of the week and have our discussion. Then on another day of the week, the whole, very large group of 500 to 1,000 women would gather in one of the larger churches and the lady who was the head of this group in the city would teach on what we had been discussing that week. It was a very effective program and I enjoyed it very much. Therefore, leading a Bible study was not foreign to me and I took it on with eagerness.

In those first few years, we held the Bible studies in homes and they were very informal. Very often, they grew rapidly and the ladies attending found it to be an effective way to get their friends around the Word of God and among other Christians. We tried to keep them free of legalism and "church" doctrine, centering in on subjects such as prayer, relationships, etc., always endeavoring to bring people closer to the Lord. Very often we would have ladies commit their lives to the Lord through this avenue. I truly found this always to be the high point of my week. I loved studying to get ready for these sessions and then delivering what I believed that the Lord had given me to the ladies. Although we were nondenominational, very often ladies from surrounding denominational churches would attend and get "hooked" on the Word. In some cases, they, with their families, started attending our church.

Therefore, home meetings, (or home fellowships, or cell meetings as they are often called today) were very ordinary to us. When we began to be invited to "charismatic" home meetings, the only thing which was strange to us was the charismatic part. We had read various books about the baptism of the Holy Spirit and had many of the same objections which we had been taught by our nondenominational, fundamental, evangelical roots. Those were the days of what is commonly called the "charismatic renewal," which took place in every major denomination and nondenominational group all over America. We fought against this Pentecostal doctrine with every argument that we had been taught. Many of those people who tried to talk to us about these things concerning tongues, healing, etc. did not know as much about the doctrines of the Word of God as we did so we could pretty much out-argue them. However, the thing that we could not combat was the love which we saw exhibited in their lives. We were familiar with the doctrines of the Word, but they had a love for Jesus and for one another which totally mystified us.

My husband was friendly, outgoing, and knowledgeable about the Word and was much less scared of the charismatic people than I was. He was open to listen to them and he felt that he had enough understanding of the Word that they couldn't get him off track or confused. From their viewpoint, they were delighted that a pastor was discussing these things with them. They kept inviting us to come to their meetings. There were Catholics, Episcopalians, Lutherans, Baptists and many others. They all just seemed to put their doctrinal differences aside and just gathered together to worship the Lord. I was terrified of the whole thing. I didn't want to go. I tried to talk my husband out of it. He, on the other hand, was curious. Finally, he told one of them that he would come to their meeting.

I remember distinctly that I was very upset that he had gone to the meeting. I made sure that I had gone to bed before he got home that evening. I, again, felt like "Something" was coming between us. Remember, my marriage and my relationship with my man was the most important thing in my life. It was actually more important to me than my relationship with the Lord. Now, I didn't think that then. I would have denied it had it been suggested. It was not likely that anyone would ever have suggested it though because I never let anyone get close enough to me for that and I never would have talked to anyone regarding these matters. I had always been a private person and our marriage relationship was private, as far as I was concerned. However, I had the distinct impression that I was being challenged to embrace what I didn't think I wanted if I was going to maintain the closeness with my husband which we had always had.

The next morning he told me all about the meeting. He told me about the home and the people. They were all just normal people. He told me about the songs they had sung. One lady had played a guitar and they had sung these scripture choruses which were quite beautiful. He said that they had begun to sing in tongues and that he had never heard anything so beautiful in his life. He then related to me how that they had all laid hands upon him and prayed for him and that he had begun to speak in tongues. He said, "You want to hear me?" He then proceeded to speak in tongues. I was aghast. I was not exactly offended by the tongues, but I was offended by the fact that we were not in harmony on this. I really was upset because I knew in my heart that we were divided on this and that I couldn't live with that. I was utterly miserable.

The following Sunday, during the day, my husband hurt his ankle very badly. By Sunday evening, it was very swollen and I was beginning to think that he had broken it. He could hardly walk. We talked and agreed that we were probably going to have to go to the doctor on Monday. On Monday morning, I was awakening from sleep and my husband brought me coffee, which was his custom. As I got my eyes open, all of a sudden, I realized that he was not limping as he had been when we went to bed. I sat up in bed and said, "What happened to your ankle?" He proceeded to tell me this story. I will tell it as I remember him telling me. He said that about 3:00 in the morning, he was awakened by hearing his name called. He thought he was imagining it and turned over to go back to sleep. Again, he heard his name audibly, as before. He began to think about Samuel, in the Bible, hearing the Lord call his name. He then talked to the Lord and asked, "Lord, is that You?" He heard these words then on the inside of himself, "Get up, I want to teach you something." He got out of bed, limped to the kitchen, got his Bible and a notebook and sat down at the table. He said, "Okay, here I am." For the next 2 hours, he was directed by the Holy Spirit from one passage of scripture to another, all dealing with the gifts of the Holy Spirit and how they were applicable today. We had always been taught that they had died out toward the end of the first century. During this lesson from the Lord, he learned otherwise. There was an emphasis on the gift of healing in this lesson from the Lord. After about 2 hours of this, he distinctly heard the Lord say on the inside of himself, "Ask Me to heal your ankle." He said he sat there very quiet for awhile and then, very formally said, "Lord, would you please heal my ankle." He said that he audibly heard a loud crack and felt something in his ankle. He was afraid to even look at his ankle. He just got up off the chair and began to walk. There was no pain. He could walk normally. He looked down and the swelling was gone.

This instantaneous miracle was not in my body but because my husband and I were so close, it had a definite impact on my life. It was right before my eyes. I could not deny it. I had to face up to the reality of all the things which I had believed were not for today's church. I could not, as an honest, thinking, logical person keep believing what I had been taught. God would do the same things today that He did in the early days of the church. This opened up a whole new world to me. I was in awe.

The next week I told him that I would go with him to the meeting. I still was scared. I told him that there had better not be one of these charismatic Christians putting hands on my head and saying or doing anything weird. I was a nervous wreck by the time I got to the meeting. Nobody was doing anything strange. They all acted like normal people. When the meeting began, and the singing started, I melted. It was so beautiful. I still have a tape of some of those scripture choruses. When they began to sing in tongues, I was awed, mystified, and a little jealous. I wanted that ability too but I was much too private a person to let anyone pray for me publicly.

A couple of weeks later, in our home, I prayed and received the baptism of the Holy Spirit, with the manifestation of speaking in tongues. Little did I know then that this miracle would prove to be so valuable to me. I saw it, at the time, as a doorway into miracles, which it was; but it was so much more also. Praying in tongues – or praying in the spirit – is the most precious gift that the Lord has ever given to me, other than my salvation. It is my constant connection, in my spirit, through the Holy Spirit, to my Heavenly Father. It is my spiritual lifeline. It is my way to pray when I don't know what to pray. It is my way of yielding to Him, when my mind doesn't know what to do. It is my Father's wonderful gift to me to constantly help me in this life, but I didn't know all that then.

Just like my husband did everything else, he jumped into this new way of believing and thinking with both feet. Before I knew what happened, we were going to home meetings all over the mountains. It seemed that we had a meeting somewhere every night. Almost from the time that my husband received the baptism and was healed, there was a gift of healing in his life. When he would get in a meeting of any kind where there was a sick person – someone who needed healing – he would seem to have an intense desire to pray for people. We didn't know about these things. We weren't sure what to do or how to handle it. However, my husband, being the type of person he was, would just start stepping out and laying hands on people and praying for them. He just expected them to be healed. We began to see people receive healing.

One evening, we had returned home late from a home meeting and I had one of the most horrible headaches that I had ever had. I sank down onto a chair at the kitchen table and he started to pray for me. The minute he touched my shoulder, the headache instantly left. It was one of the most startling experiences for me. When you have had horrible pain, and then suddenly it is gone, you're afraid to move. You're afraid it will come back. You keep expecting it to hurt and it's gone. I was utterly amazed.

I truly believed that this baptism in the Holy Spirit was the answer to all the problems we had known in our lives up to that point. I saw, of course, that it was the doorway into the miraculous. I thought that living the Christian life, which had always seemed so hard, would certainly be a snap now. If you could ask for and receive miracles, if you could get broken ankles and headaches healed, then overcoming fleshly desires which were against the Word of God ought to be easy now. I really thought that this baptism in the Holy Spirit was going to help us walk through our lives in a godly manner. I really did not understand that the "power" was in the tongues to pray – that the "power" of the gifts of the Spirit was to help people, like Jesus did. I did not understand that living the Christian life is a moment by moment walk of grace, trusting what Jesus has already done. The victorious Christian life is a life lived with the awareness that your "old self" has died on the cross with Jesus, and that the new life in you is the Jesus life in you. I was expecting that, since we both had the baptism in the Holy Spirit, that the Holy Spirit was going to control us now and we wouldn't have the "flesh" battles which had been such a problem. My husband believed that also. It was a sad day in our home when we found out that was not true. It seemed that "Yo-Yo Christianity," was not over for us. Here's all this power and we still had the same problems. We wanted to live the victorious Christian life but it seemed that my husband went from highs to lows. He would have wonderful things happen through the gifts of the Spirit and he loved to minister the Word. All of the new life in the Spirit was exciting but yielding to the flesh always seemed to bring on a bout of feeling very bad and feeling like victory would never be his. That, of course, brought on a "defeated" attitude and more problems. I cared deeply for him but I didn't know how to make it any different. The only thing I knew to do was stand by him in the midst of his problem until he came out on the other side – which he always did.

CHAPTER FOUR

DEMONS – OH NO!!

In the midst of the charismatic renewal with its obvious interest in the supernatural, there was an increased awareness of demonic activity. When one begins to study the Word of God with a childlike attitude towards the New Testament, a new appreciation for the teachings of Jesus naturally follows. The New Testament has much to say about the power of the Holy Spirit. It also has much to say about the works of the enemy of God, the devil. To accept what it says about God and His power and yet to ignore what it says about who our enemy is and what he tries to do in our lives is not a logical or wise attitude. Along with this increased knowledge came many, many teachers giving information to Christians who, up to that time, had been ignorant in this realm. For many, many people, learning about these things for the first time was fascinating. When you have studied the Bible for years, and your knowledge has primarily been in the field of doctrines, with the doctrine of salvation being the only area where you could actually experience God, this was awesome. Most of us, in those years of which I am speaking, had pretty much been grounded in the fact that salvation was by grace through faith. It was not an emotional experience. There could be emotions involved but your salvation was not based on emotions, or feelings, but on the Word of God. All of that is true. I still believe that!

What began to occur in Charismatic circles is an awareness of the devil as a real personality in this earth with a plan and purpose to defeat Christians. There began to be much activity centering around teaching Christians to live victoriously over the devil. Of course, in order to live victoriously, one had to get the devil out of one's life. Therefore, there was much "casting out."

As I reflect on these things, I really believe that many of us saw this as a way we could "do" something. So much of the Christian life was a faith issue and now we were being told that we could actually do something ourselves. We could cast him out. We began to look, as someone has said, "for a demon behind every bush." We saw every wrong action and every wrong word as an indication of the presence of the enemy. Ministries sprang up overnight, it seemed, with an emphasis on casting out demons.

I must tell you that I was very reluctant to embrace this new facet of the Pentecostal life. However, that was my attitude each step of the way, it seemed, in spiritual things. We had almost gotten used to my husband always jumping on the bandwagon of each new avenue of thinking and me holding back. It seemed that he always had to pull me into new things with me kicking and screaming all the way. You understand, I hope, that I don't mean that literally. I just mean that I never really wanted to go into these new areas but he did and so, in order for us to not be divided in anything, I would always give in.

I have always been a reader so I began to read books written by some of these teachers who had come on the scene. I began to form an opinion, much like the one I was sure that my husband had formed. Perhaps this was the answer that we had been looking for all these years. Maybe victory over the flesh, victory in the Christian life, walking in the spirit was so hard because the devil had prevented it. There is a joking phrase which has become quite common in recent years and most generally brings a smile to the face – "the devil made me do it." Quite literally, this became the emphasis during that period of time in many lives.

Let me say now, in a very simple statement, that the devil is very much at work in this world. He hates God and will do whatever he can to prevent God's work, to hinder God's people, to cause problems, calamities, etc. in the lives of both believers and nonbelievers.

I do believe that he does possess people, oppress people, and harass people all over the world. I want to make it clear that I see from the Word of God that we, as believers, in Jesus' name have the power to exercise our authority over him and I do so at every opportunity. However, I have come to believe that the human will is extremely powerful. We, ourselves, have the power to reject evil in our lives. If we are very careful to study the way Jesus dealt with the devil, with sickness, with infirmity, with lack (either bodily or materially) He depended on the Holy Spirit to know when there was an evil spirit there and when there was not. Every situation is not the same. Jesus did not look for a "demon behind every bush."

At that time, however, there was often more emphasis on casting him out than on worshipping Jesus. Throughout the charismatic circles, in both churches and home meetings, there were "casting out" services. There were books written. Every conceivable problem that any person had ever encountered was now considered to be the result of demon activity. The logical conclusion then was – get rid of the demon, get rid of the problem. Therefore, deliverance meetings became common. I am sure that the devil enjoyed getting so much attention during those years. My husband went through "deliverance," and was pronounced free from all demonic activity. Whoopee! I thought we really had hit on the answer this time. This had to be it. No more ups and downs! No more trips into the world! We'd just be spiritual all the time and live the way the New Testament instructed us to live. That mind-set lasted about two to three months – until the next problem in life came along. We found out that we still had some of those same problems.

The wonderful life of grace which the Lord has provided for us in Christ is a life free from law, free from works, and free from religion. It is a life in which one says, "Lord, my old self is dead. My old self died on the cross with Jesus. A dead man can do nothing. A dead man can't talk. You are now in me. You are now my life. I only do what You do. I only say what You say." As long as we keep trying to live for God, trying to live the Christian life, trying to do the right thing, we will struggle. Some people struggle all their lives. My husband did.

We must realize that we live the Christian life the same way that we get saved in the first place – by grace through faith – and that not of ourselves. (Eph. 2:8) There is absolutely no difference between us "trying" to live the Christian life with our new resolutions, our new commitments, our turning over a new leaf, our attempt to be holy, than there was with the early church and their tendency to go back into rules, regulations, and religion. The Apostle Paul dealt with this considerably in Galatians, Colossians, and many other places in other letters. When we try in our flesh (our own abilities or strengths) to live the Christian life, we will fail. When we attempt to find any other thing, even something spiritual, to help us live the Christian life, we will fail. The Christian life is impossible for us to live. It can only be lived by the Jesus life (the new you). That is the whole mystery of the New Testament – Christ in you, the hope of glory! (Col. 1:27)

But we didn't know all that then. We were disillusioned. We were so tired of trying. The world is full of Christians who are tired of trying. We had had some successes in ministry. We had seen many people saved, healed, filled with the Holy Spirit and we enjoyed the ministry. However, we did not enjoy trying to live the Christian life. We were constantly falling short of what we thought the Lord expected of us and what we expected of ourselves.

We left our church, moved our family back to our hometown and both of us took secular jobs. We attended church here and there. We went to some denominational churches which did not believe in miracles, healing, and the baptism in the Holy Spirit. As you might expect, we were forever spoiled by the miraculous. We wandered for awhile. We went to some denominational, full-gospel churches but we had been non-denominational for so long that we could not deal with denominations at all, even full-gospel ones. Every place we would go, the pastor or an elder would try to talk us in to getting involved in that church. It was as though my husband was wearing a big sign around his neck, saying, "I Am a Pastor – I Have Been in the Ministry!" We would try to hide out but we couldn't seem to carry it out very well. Of course, I know now that a call on a life cannot stay hidden very long.

CHAPTER FIVE

PLEASE GOD! BRING MY DAUGHTER HOME

We were now living back in our hometown and our children were both teenagers. They had been through the ups and downs of Bible School, churches, the mountains, the baptism in the Holy Spirit, the fascination with demons, in and out of the ministry, etc. with us. We were a very close family. Both of our kids always had the awareness that Mom and Dad loved each other. They always knew that Mom would always stick by Dad and that Dad would always stick by Mom. They also recognized that being in and out of the ministry and in and out of secular employment had taken a toll on us. It had also taken a toll on our kids, especially on our daughter. When we had been running all over the mountains to all those home meetings, enjoying ourselves so much in our new-found "power of the Holy Spirit," our daughter was in her pre-junior high school age and needed us at home more than we were. We were too self-centered and caught up with how the Lord might use us to realize it then. Through those years, we were losing our daughter and we didn't even know it.

Well, we didn't think we would do it again but we did. We went back in the ministry. This time, we started a church. We started it on Sunday evenings in our home. We had a large family room and some Sunday evenings we had as many as 60 to 70 people packed in there. We had the "nursery" in a bedroom and had coffee and goodies in the kitchen and dining area for after the meeting. We had portable music. We had wall-to-wall people. We had my husband's office in the home also and it seemed as though we had a steady stream of people through there each week. What a lot of cleaning and preparation this all took. We had both quit our jobs and were "trusting the Lord," to see to us and our family. We really outgrew the house fairly quickly and began to meet in a community center in our area. There was quite a bit of work involved there as well, carrying everything in before services on Sunday and out afterwards. There was space for Sunday School and Nursery and, of course, that involved more "stuff."

Through this period of time, we came across some teaching which was quite different from anything we had ever heard before. I will never forget the first time we heard this message. My husband and I were in the car. We tried to take some time each week to just go on a drive, go out to eat and, generally, just relax. We were listening to a tape by a man with whom we were not familiar. However, I will never forget what he said on that tape. This man said, and proved it from the Scriptures, that God was a good God and that He wanted good things for His children. Now up to that time, we had sometimes gotten prayers answered here and there. When we had success with prayer, we never knew what had caused it to work that time. It was rather hit and miss. We always tacked on, "If it be Thy will," because we never knew what was His will and what was not. This preacher was telling us on this tape that God was not a big ogre up there in heaven pushing out cancer and earthquakes on His children. He was telling us that if we would study the Word, we could know what the will of God was and that if we would pray according to the will of God, we could always get our prayers answered. Well, we considered ourselves Word people. We had begun to study the Word the same week my husband was saved all those years before. We were absolutely dumb-founded. We had never heard preaching or teaching like that before. We went to a park, sat in the car and listened to that tape again. In the next 36 hours, we listened to every one of the tapes in the series which had been loaned to us. (About 12 tapes!) We listened again and again.

What wonderful news!

We set about getting every tape we could afford to get by this preacher and others who were preaching the same message. We were like children with a new toy. We had a new message. God was a good God! This just opened up all kinds of avenues of thinking to us. We talked and talked and talked. We saw where our thinking had been influenced by religion, rather than the Word. Here my husband had a Bible School degree in Biblical Education but we had never heard anyone say these things before. Never had anyone offered real answers to questions which had always lingered around in the back of our minds concerning the nature of God and prayer. This message seemed to cause us to see the Word from the standpoint of God loving us and desiring to help us rather than from a religious standpoint. We began to look at the words and works of Jesus differently. We began to think about expressing faith in the Word of God – believing that God would do what He said He would do. We began to think about faith as believing it before seeing it. We began to see that our prayers through the years had primarily been "hoping and praying," instead of "believing and receiving" before seeing.

What a change in thinking this was! We felt like we were babies in these things. My husband began to teach these things as quickly as he was learning them. We certainly weren't grounded in them but we were so excited about the truths we were learning that we wanted to share them with everyone coming to our church.

During this period of time, our daughter had gotten further and further away from us. She was frustrated in her own self and going through the trauma of the teen years. Of course, the drug scene and all of the things which go along with rebellion, frustration, hurt, anxiety, etc. began to work overtime in her life. She left home several times in a relatively brief period of time. It was an extremely difficult time for all of us. Each of us, in our own way, was hurt and feeling a great deal of pain. I was so full of guilt and feeling like a failure as a parent, and was also so hurt and angry at her for what I perceived as her wounding us so deeply. I just didn't see how she could do this to us, being the close family we had always been. My husband was terribly embarrassed by the whole thing and very angry at her. He felt like she was making us look really bad and that she should know better. He saw it as a personal attack on us as we tried to get the church going. He loved her dearly but he just wanted her to come to her senses and quit making such a big problem. Our son, about a year older than her, tried to stay in the middle of the road – he knew how we felt and, in some ways, felt the same way; but, he also knew her so well, in some ways better than we did. He was hurting for her through this. You know, close siblings can sometimes be each other's worst enemy and other times be each other's dearest friend.

During that time, there were weeks when we did not hear from her. We would hear little bits and pieces here and there and we knew that things were not good. It was a time filled with extreme worry, anger, and fear. We did not know if she had food to eat or if she was warm. The fear, at times, was overwhelming. My husband and I cried together and hung on to each other, trying to convince each other that it would turn out okay. Then she would call and after two or three words out of her mouth, we would be so angry. My husband would be angry at her for what she was putting me through. I would try to calm him down. It was total frustration.

BUT ――― we had heard that God was a good God and that we could know what His will was. We had heard that we could pray, according to His will, and that He would hear and answer us. We practically spent every waking hour studying the Word. We looked up every verse in the Word that had anything to say about our children. We read New Testament verses and Old Testament verses. We studied and we read. We talked and talked and talked. We talked through our frustrations. We admitted our failures to the Lord and we asked Him to give us revelation concerning these things. After I began to become convinced that God would bring my daughter back home and that her mind was being blinded by the enemy (2 Cor. 4:4-5), I got mad. Mad at the devil – instead of mad at my daughter! We knew that down deep inside was that sweet little girl we had raised – that she just couldn't see things clearly – but that if we would believe the promises in the Word of God and then pray for our daughter, God would speak to her and bring her back to Himself and to us.

We wrote every verse down that showed us what God would do

for us regarding our daughter, and showing our authority in the name of Jesus. We could practically quote all of them without looking at the Bible because we had studied so intently. We made up our minds that we were going to do all our talking before we prayed because after we prayed, we were only going to pray in the Spirit for our daughter and thank and praise the Lord that He was working in her life. You see, we were taking this very seriously. As far as we were concerned, it was a matter of life and death – our daughter's. We covenanted together (made an agreement together) that from the moment we prayed, we would not let one word escape our lips which was contrary to what we believed that God was doing in our daughter's life.

We set a time for our praying. We took the phone off the hook and got somewhere where we couldn't see if someone came to the door. We committed to each other that we would not be disturbed. We got our Bibles and our notes and we began to pray. We prayed everything on our hearts until we were all prayed out. It was not a two-minute prayer. When we were finished, we began to thank the Lord for hearing and answering us. We praised Him and prayed and sang in the Spirit.

Then the real test of faith began. Nothing changed! The first week, the second week, the third week all went by. Still no change! I remember one night, sitting in the tub, taking a bath, and the overwhelming ache for my daughter threatened to do me in. The thoughts of, "Will I ever hold my baby again?" were screaming on the inside of me. I sat there in the tub, sobbing in my bath water, praying in tongues, not letting a word of unbelief come out of my mouth. I believe that, at that moment, I had the victory. The victory did not come when I was all fired up when we first prayed. The victory came when everything was screaming at me in the natural, human realm to not believe that God had heard me and had answered me the moment I prayed. I was fighting for my daughter's life. I was believing God!

Some weeks later, the Lord brought her home to us. There were some natural circumstances which were the avenues through which God worked but no one could ever convince me that my Heavenly Father had not heard and answered the prayers from the hearts of a mother and a father. A few days after she had come back to us, we were having a church service in the community center and my husband was giving an invitation. Our daughter came running to the front, threw herself in her daddy's arms and said, "I want to come back to you and to Jesus." There was not a dry eye in church that day. Truly, God is good. Such a wrong picture has been painted about Him and it has invaded the church, big time! The world calls earthquakes, hurricanes, tornadoes, and all sorts of natural catastrophes "acts of God." They don't know that there is an enemy of God, the devil, who is rampaging through the universe doing horrible things to God's beautiful creation and to man, the very best of God's creation. However, the church, who says that, "God so loved the world that He sent His only begotten Son, that whosoever believeth in Him should not perish but have everlasting life," (John 3:16) ought to know better. Yes, God is a good God!

CHAPTER SIX

THEY ACTUALLY LISTEN WHEN I TEACH!

My husband and I had both become accustomed to operating in the gifts of the Spirit (spiritual gifts) mentioned in 1 Cor. 12. We had learned the difference between praying to the Lord in tongues and delivering a message in tongues from the Lord, which requires an interpretation. We had begun to learn that prayer in tongues was a powerful gift that the Holy Spirit had given us when we had received the baptism in the Holy Spirit. We found out that, as we prayed in tongues, many good things were the result. We could pray for others. No one human being knows what is in the heart of another and, consequently, we need the help of the Holy Spirit to pray the perfect will of God for others as it talks about in Rom. 8. Praying in tongues, or in the Spirit, accomplishes what we cannot with our limited human knowledge. Another good thing about praying in tongues, we learned, was that we could be built up (or charged up) within ourselves as it talks about in Jude. We discovered that praying in tongues was the only way that we could do as the Apostle Paul had instructed in 1 Thes. 5:17, "Pray without ceasing." We found that the more time we spent praying in tongues, the more "in tune," we were with the Lord and the more that the gifts of the Holy Spirit would flow. More power, more healings, etc. seemed to be the result.

We found that the Lord would often give us direction during these times of prayer. One day, while spending time in this kind of praying, the Lord directed us to go to a certain area and told us that there would be a building which we would be able to buy and use for a church building. He gave us specifics, which we had no way of knowing in the natural realm. We did as He directed us and, within weeks, were doing the work necessary to move into our own building. There were many such ways in which He led us.

During this period of time, the church was growing and we were very involved in the ministry of the Word of God. I had started a daytime women's Bible study. We would put our chairs in a big circle and I would minister whatever I felt like the Lord wanted for us to study. I remember, distinctly, the day that the Lord told me, ahead of the meeting, that He wanted me to stand up and teach. When I say that He told me, I do not mean that I heard an audible voice. I had learned that, as I prayed a lot in the Spirit, I became very sensitive to what the Lord wanted in specific ways. It was an inner knowing. It was not figuring something out with natural, human reasoning. It was coming from somewhere deep within me, coming to my mind, and I just knew. I knew things that I hadn't known before. That's what this was. I was deeply aware that the Lord was asking me to place the chairs in rows, like church or school and stand before them to teach them. I was petrified. That might sound silly to you but I was genuinely very scared. It seemed to me that, as long as we sat in a circle, I was just leading a Bible study; but if I stood in front of them, I was taking the position of a teacher. That opened up all kinds of avenues of thought for me, and I was scared of them all. I regarded my position as a helper to my husband. He was a pastor. I was his helper. I figured that if he weren't a pastor, I wouldn't be doing this teaching. Somehow, within me, to stand before a group of people and teach was to declare that I believed that God had gifted me to teach. My dilemma was that if I did not believe that God had gifted me to teach, then why was I doing it and enjoying it so much – actually studying and planning all week for this one session? Why did it matter so much to me? Why were these classes growing so much and so many people being helped in the things of God?

I struggled with these questions. I didn't have the feeling that God would be upset with me if I chose to do it the way I had been – I just felt as though I was at a crossroads and that He was putting something new before me. I didn't want people to think that I thought that I was a big deal. I didn't want to give the impression that I felt like I had suddenly become very important. I struggled! At last, I told the Lord that I would do as I believed He was asking me to do and I would leave the, "What will people think?" to Him. That first time, I was very nervous but I discovered that when I began to teach what was on the inside of me with the motivation of helping the people understand what I had gotten a hold of, my nervousness began to fade and I was totally consumed with the need of getting this out of me to the people. As the weeks went by, I became aware that I had a "knowing" in me when they were getting it and when they weren't. I found that the Lord would give me ways of expressing myself to get a point across. I began to lose self-consciousness when I was teaching and I also began to have ideas about what to teach which seemed to be exactly what the people needed. The little class began to grow. As had occurred before, people who were invited to the class who were not a part of our church would often end up coming to the regular services of the church. The Lord seemed to use my Bible teaching to bring families into the church. Many were saved and filled with the Holy Spirit. It was not easy for me to pray for people to be healed. I was familiar with the gift of healing which operated through my husband but I had no awareness of it operating through me. The Bible says in Mark 16 that believers, "will lay hands on the sick and they will recover." Therefore, I did pray for people to be healed in obedience to that verse of scripture.

I began to notice that when I would teach the Word of God, it was like I became another person. I had always been shy and quiet, but, when I was teaching, I could talk and talk, with absolutely no fear, hammering something home until I "knew" they had gotten it. It seemed so strange to the way I had always been. People close to me would tease me about me "getting the 'preach' on me." We would laugh but it would trouble me also because that made me sound like a woman preacher. I began to study the Word in this regard. If it was wrong, why did it seem so right? I still saw myself as a helper to my husband and, when things were said that put me in the category of a teacher or a preacher, I didn't know how to handle it.

I also had another twist to this situation for which I needed answers. People were beginning to compare the way my husband ministered the Word to the way I ministered the Word. My husband had been trained in Bible School. He had learned all the ways to prepare sermons. He had training in exposition, exegesis, and lots of other things which I didn't understand. I didn't know anything about all of the correct ways to put a message together. I didn't consider what I said, when I stood before people, delivering a sermon anyway. I saw it as giving out to others what the Lord had given to me. I did not struggle to come up with something to teach. I could not open my Bible without having questions popping up in me which required me to get a concordance and look up words in the Hebrew and Greek. When I would find the answers I searched for, I would jot down an outline with some scripture verses and I would be ready to teach it. It was not an effort. It seemed that people were being helped to understand the Word.

I tried to make sure that I did not see myself as on the same ministerial level as my husband. I regarded him as the pastor and me as his helper. I encouraged him. I praised him. I absolutely never criticized him, and I never said anything negative about him to others, even in teasing or joking. We had always had a habit pattern over the years of never jokingly putting each other down around other people. We saw so many married people be critical of each other and, if they said things laughingly, it was supposed to be all right. We never did that. No one ever heard us talk negatively about one another, even our children. I tried to make absolutely sure that I listened closely to everything that he preached and looked for good things that I could comment on and praise. My husband would always have a healing, or ministry, line after preaching and that healing power would seem to always be present. Therefore, the way that I found to deal with this comparison problem was to always keep an emphasis on his strong gift and make light of whatever I did. I so did not want him to be hurt. I didn't want him to feel like he didn't measure up. He was the one who had spent 5 years in

Bible School. I had noticed that, when he began to feel like he didn't measure up it had the effect on him of his flesh trying to have the preeminence and we would always end up with problems.

My Bible class was growing and there were men occasionally coming. It was big enough that, when we had moved into our own building, I was having the class in the auditorium area in which we had church. Therefore, since I was ministering from the platform, behind the pulpit, and wearing a microphone (because people had begun to want to buy tapes), I was becoming more familiar with the whole process of teaching people. One man, in particular, came often and approached me one day after the class. He said that he believed that I should be on Christian radio and that if I would agree to it, he would pay a considerable amount in the beginning to get it all going. I was flabbergasted! I had a whole range of emotions at this proposal. I was scared - excited – flattered – and very nervous about telling my husband. I knew that I didn't know how to do all that but I really wanted to do it. I knew that the mechanics of the whole thing would be right up my husband's alley. He would know how to do it all. But—-I didn't want him to feel like I was being sought after to teach the Word, and he was not; that I was being given opportunities, and he was not. I very carefully, trying to not show too much excitement, shared all this conversation with my husband. He was positively elated. He did not act as though he was bothered at all that it was me and not him who was being asked to do this. I carefully brought up the subject, tactfully trying to have an honest discussion about it before we went another step. He assured me, I believe, from the bottom of his heart, that if they had asked me, they had asked him – because we were one. He told me that he knew that I had been given a gift by God to teach the Word and he wanted to do everything he could to help me in any way possible. That was a very special moment. I loved him so much as he said these things to me. I felt like we made the decision together for me to embark on this radio ministry and we began to take the first steps. My husband truly knew how to do all the things that I didn't know how to do to make it work. All I had to do was teach.

Following that conversation about me teaching, my husband began to have me minister the Word from the pulpit occasionally during our regular services. This was certainly another step for me. I had actually become what I had always distanced myself from being known as – a woman preacher. Oh well – I am what I am! I have since discovered that many women called by God to have public ministries have gone through some of these same agonizing mental traumas.

Going on the radio caused the church to become known in our area and people began to come who had not come before. I began to receive speaking invitations from various places, both in and around our community and from further away. It was a very exciting time for me. I was so excited that God really wanted to use me to help people. During this period of time, my husband and I began to do what we called, "team teaching." It is a common husband and wife ministry today but then we didn't know of anyone else who was doing it. Because I was invited to do different kinds of meetings, there were opportunities for us to minister together. We found that we could follow an outline and talk from that outline in a way that people seemed to enjoy and learn from. We were so in tune with each other that we "flowed" together well in this type of teaching. I liked it because I could include my husband in this "expanded" ministry. I felt like it was good for him. Things were very good. However, I must say that always lurking in the corner recesses of my being was the knowledge that the "flesh" was always right there ready to spring out when least expected and cause everything to come tumbling down. However, since I did not know what to do about that, I tried to put that out of my mind. I thought I was just being negative in my thinking.

CHAPTER SEVEN

AND THE WALLS CAME TUMBLING DOWN

B ecause of my husband's intense desire to be successful in the ministry, he was always looking for something to "put him over," as so many ministers are. Also, because of "the only success-ful church is a large church" mentality, which was fast becoming part of Christian thinking, my husband felt like he just had to find a way to make the church big quickly and was susceptible to decep-tion. Because of that deception, he did not make wise choices in some of his interactions with people. One unwise choice seems to lead to more unwise choices.

As I reflect on those years in as honest a way as I can and as the Lord has enabled me to see, my husband was desperately trying to find his "niche" in life. I firmly believe with all my heart that the Lord never intended for the ministry to become a "profession" as it has become in the church today. I know that the Word teaches that those who labor in the Word should be supported financially by those whom they teach. I believe that! However, today's church has become so accustomed to a ministry very far removed from what it was in the early church. We, like so many Christians, saw the ministry as a profession to go into – a career. My husband was a bright, intelligent, talented man. The Lord also gave him gifts, which, because he loved people and wanted to help them, operated very powerfully. He was deeply compassionate in dealing with people who were hurting terribly with the blows of life. However, when God gives us gifts, they are never to put us over; never to help us; never to give us a life, a profession, a ministry. They aren't for us. It isn't about us. It's all about Jesus. I believe that there are countless numbers of wounded men and women floating around in the earth today, not knowing where they belong – disillusioned, frustrated, and angry because they tried to do something for God and it didn't work. They had gifts from the Lord and they embarked on a profession – a career – a lifestyle of the ministry, and then they had to keep on trying to perform to be successful.

When poor judgment is exercised by a person who is in spiritual authority, problems are unavoidable. When you lose people, you lose money. When you have made financial commitments based on a certain amount of money, which of necessity is based on a certain amount of people, and the people aren't there, something not good is going to happen. The radio time was the first thing to go. We couldn't afford it. Over the next couple of years, we tried just about everything we could to keep things going. My husband was facing extreme trauma within himself. His innermost being was in turmoil. His life was in a circle which he couldn't seem to control. Let me see if I can explain it. He was very happy for the success in ministering the Word of God which I was having and he was very proud of me. But deep on the inside of him, he felt that the success we had been enjoying in our ministry was not because of him. It made him feel empty inside because the ministry was his profession. He was supposed to be taking care of me, he felt. He was the man! Therefore, because he felt empty, and unimportant (no matter how much I tried to build up his ego), it took him further downhill until he began to think like a natural man, not a spiritual man. Thus, in some instances, he exercised poor judgment. Then the feeling of defeat set in. The very thing which had brought much of the success and he had been so proud of – the radio program – was the first thing to go. He felt like he had failed me.

From my point of view during this time, I just couldn't believe that we couldn't revive things and make it still work. I have sense described that period of time as trying to make a dead horse get up off the ground and run again. The church was the dead horse. We tried changing our living situation so that money requirements were less, but no matter what we did, nothing worked. It was dead. I just didn't want to believe it. I tried to pray and pray and pray. There were so many things wrong and so many emotions involved and so many problems which there seemed to be no answer for that each day was a horrible period of time to just be gotten through somehow and maybe sleep would come. We spent hours and hours talking. My husband felt like he had let God down, me down, our children down, the church down, everybody he knew in the world down! To be very honest, I struggled with feeling like he had let us all down too. Mostly me! There was a period of time in there when he did not want to continue to live.

He absolutely did not feel like he could stay in the ministry. He felt like a total failure – and yes, I felt like he had ruined everything. I felt like, through no fault of my own, I was being forced into being a "Yo-Yo" again.

I remember the night that I weighed everything in my mind very carefully. Through torturous struggling, I made a decision. I would not continue to fight my husband about closing the church and him getting a secular job. I wanted to move away from the area as soon as possible. We were known pretty well in the community and, being the private person that I was, I was being tormented by the thought of constantly running into people. I decided that I would not pursue the ministry, even though I had the distinct impression that if I were not associated with my husband, I could do so successfully. I absolutely could not face life without my man. Looking deep within myself, I honestly told the Lord that my marriage to my man was more important to me than ministering to people. I cannot tell you how agonizing this was for me. I really loved to minister the Word of God. I remember the exact moment that I told the Lord all these things, laying on a couch in a dark living room, feeling a little dead inside as I said them. I felt like I had just made a choice to end some of the most wonderful things which I had ever experienced in life. To never teach the Word again! To never feel the exhilaration of being an instrument of bringing revelation knowledge to people and see the "light-bulb" go on in them, when they "get it!" I didn't think I could stand it. But I knew I would. I had to.

I knew I was leaving the ministry to be with my husband – and that is as it should have been. However, where I missed it, I should have prayed us both back to where we were supposed to be. I knew how to pray to change things. However, emotionally, I just gave up. I just didn't think I could do anymore or take anymore. I was defeated!

The next few years are rather nondescript in many ways. We had some fun times; but as I ponder now, purpose and meaning, for the most part, died in my husband when he left the ministry. He tried to fill that void with interest in other things. He never was mad at God. Mad at himself, yes! It took a long time for that to quiet down in him. It was so bad for awhile that he could not look at our family albums because they were filled with pictures of ministry things – his graduation from Bible School, his ordination, people from the churches where we pastored. I knew very clearly what decision I had made and why I had made it. I also was very much aware that the Lord knew exactly where I was, why I was there, and what was going on in my life. I tried to give my husband what I believed that he needed – my love, my understanding, my compassion, and my faithfulness. I knew that no one in the whole world knew him like I did, except the Lord. I knew, down in the core of his being, he loved the Lord and really just felt like he had messed up both of our lives, as well as failed the Lord. I gave him all that I had to give – myself. Because I loved him!

I have come to see, though, that my husband led me step by step into the deeper things of God. I was the type of personality that would have held back. In fact, I did. Because of him, though, and his persistence, and because I did not ever want anything to divide us, I have come into all the wonderful truths of the Word and the revelation knowledge that I have today. I have to say that, as I ponder these things, God's grace has constantly been my companion.

Many things changed in those years. People get older. Deaths and births occur in all our families. My husband felt a bit displaced in life. In different situations in which we found ourselves, I would catch him trying to "pastor" people. He wouldn't even realize he was doing it. Going to church was very hard. I think I have a vague idea what people feel like who have had to flee their country for one reason or another and just never feel like they fit in again. It seemed that no matter where we were, we "knew too much" to ever just go along with the program. Being out of the will of God, for a man or a woman of God, is the most horrible of all places to be. It is complete misery. We had some answered prayers during those years. My husband had a greater concept of the grace of God, even out of the will of God, than most Christians in churches have today. His attitude was essentially this, "God is my Father. I am His child. His Word declares that He loves me with unconditional love. Jesus has paid the price for me. All of my sins were future when Jesus died on the cross; therefore, they are all paid for. The sin question is settled. I will ask this of Him, and He will do it for me because He loves me. I am not good enough for Him to do this for me. I could never be good enough. Jesus was good enough and I am in Him. He loves me and that's just all there is to it."

That, my friend, is grace!

With that kind of trust in the Lord, when my husband prayed concerning a family matter, the weather, or the healing of someone's body (which happened frequently, even in those years), I knew it was a done deal.

CHAPTER EIGHT

WE DIDN'T KNOW HOW TO BE SICK!

I had begun to notice that my husband was losing weight. I also noticed that he did not have the appetite that he used to have. Even through these years out of the will of God, my husband's faith for healing was strong. He almost never went to the doctor; not because of any reason except that he just didn't feel like he needed to go. His blood pressure was always good; his heart was good; he had no cholesterol problems; and, for the most part, pretty much controlled his body. When he had learned the authority of Jesus' name and that sickness was not from God, as far as he was concerned, that was it. When flu viruses were going around, he would simply say that they weren't coming on him. He wasn't trying to convince himself or anyone else of this. He just meant it from his heart. If he began to feel a little bit bad, he would "command" whatever it was to leave him, tell his body that it was well and that it was not going to be sick, and then he would pray and thank the Lord that healing belonged to him. He then would proceed to "act" well. There were a few times through the years when something slipped up on him but I could probably count them on one hand. For the most part, he was a well man.

When he began to eat less than he had before, I attributed it to him controlling his own body and not wanting to be overweight, which, of course, we all know, brings on health problems. I had learned through all the years of marriage that, if he was involved in some sort of "faith" battle in the physical realm, he did not really want to discuss it. Therefore, a habit pattern had developed of not talking about his health problems, if there were any. I was a different story. I had health problems here and there and, if I needed to go to the doctor, I went.

Reflecting on these things now, I believe that so much of what my husband had held dear to him, he felt, had gone by the wayside. So much of his self-esteem and his self-worth had been left back there a few years ago that it seemed that the only thing he continued to hold on to was his ability to "believe God" for his own body. To tell you the truth, I really wasn't concerned. He had always handled his own health matters and I wasn't used to getting involved. It never really dawned on me that he really had a problem. I don't think it dawned on him either. He didn't feel bad. If he had "felt" it or "seen" it, I am convinced that he would have experienced victory over it.

I began to notice that he seemed to have some difficulty breathing. I mentioned it a little here and there and he pretty much "phew-phewed" the idea. However, in a relatively short period of time, it began to get worse and worse. Very quickly, there were times when he could hardly get his breath. I began to talk to him about getting a chest x-ray. It was like talking to a brick wall. In his mind, he just didn't run to doctors. I know this sounds silly and illogical but I'm trying to convey truth here, and that's the truth! He wasn't afraid. However, almost on a daily basis, the problem began to increase. Each day, it began to get worse. I saw a tiny glimmer of fear in my husband. One day, it was very bad and he decided that he would go to get a chest x-ray. He was immediately admitted to the hospital and was treated with oxygen on a continual basis while tests were run. Within days, we were given the news that my husband had an incurable lung disease which he and I had never heard of before and with which we were unfamiliar.

He was dismissed from the hospital and he began the trek of going to specialists and being treated with drugs; however, we were told from the beginning that the drugs could not cure the problem and that surgery was not an option as far as a cure was concerned.

Exploratory surgery might give some information but would probably not help the actual disease. Just in a matter of days, he could not breathe without oxygen. Therefore, just in a matter of days, our world had turned upside down.

We were working in team employment – what else for a couple like us? At this point, it was all on my shoulders. I had so many problems to consider that I really felt like I could only just put one foot in front of the other to make it through the next hour. I had money problems, job problems, where-to-live problems (because our apartment was provided with our employment), and a husband who was confined to his chair in the living room, with an oxygen tank beside him. These were truly the biggest problems I had ever encountered and I just didn't know what to do except to run to Papa God.

My husband, almost from the day that he first went in the hospital, began to seek the Lord about all these things. Within a very short period of time, he had talked to the Lord about everything in his life which he felt like was "out of kilter." He repented until his "repenter" was just about worn out. You must understand that being diagnosed with this disease did something down in him that nothing else had ever been able to do. He had fear now. He had always known, from the day that he was saved, that God loved him and then, as he grew in the grace and revelation of the Lord, he grew in his awareness of that love and what God would do for him. But he, all of a sudden, saw that because he had not stayed close to the things of God, the Word of God, the ministry of God, the Spirit of God and the church of God, something had been slipped in on him and he didn't see it coming. He knew that God hadn't made him sick, but this wasn't about warding off a virus or something of that nature. This was already entrenched, and he was afraid. He began to study the Word with fervor. He began to pray. He prayed for everybody he had ever known in his life and he prayed fervently.

I carried on the work, trying to work out what we were going to do and where we were going to go. I also took care of him. The medication he was on gave him a ferocious appetite so I spent much time on meals along with all my other duties. After dinner in the evenings, we studied the Word together and prayed together. We would not allow ourselves to speak words of death. When those thoughts would come, they were so foreign to me that I would dismiss them. You might think that I was living in a kind of fantasy world, and, to some extent, I probably was. I just didn't know how to do anything any different and I was so tired most of the time that I was doing good to just get everything done. The one thing I didn't know then, was most ignorant of, and certainly wasn't counting on, was the fear that had taken up residence with my husband. I saw little glimmers of it now and then, when he couldn't breathe, but I didn't realize how much he feared that he was not going to be able to get his healing.

Also, he was so terribly embarrassed by the whole thing. He felt like here he was, a man who had prayed for many, many people and seen them healed, and yet he was "connected" to an oxygen tank to be able to get his next breath. He didn't want people to see him this way. He didn't want even family to see him. He was very careful to not be in a picture if someone had a camera around. He knew that he looked like only a shadow of the man that he used to be and he was embarrassed about his appearance. He felt horribly bad that I was having to take care of him, make the living, etc. He felt like an invalid and he detested it. He didn't blame anyone other than himself for his condition, but he did blame himself. A large percentage of the people in the world, both Christians and non-Christians, just take sickness and disease as a part of life and figure that the odds are that they are going to be sick before they die. My husband did not believe that way and, besides that, he was not an old man. He believed that he had allowed this attack on his body and he was having trouble dealing with it.

This went on for several months. We were getting ready to move to another location and were, in fact, doing a little of the moving ourselves on the weekends. I was having to do it all really because he could not even really carry something to the car and get back to the living room without not being able to get his breath, even with the oxygen. I was also having to do all the driving. There were times through those days that his limbs would be affected and he would have pain which seemed to be very bad. I was doing all I knew to do. When those bad times of pain would occur, the only thing which seemed to bring him relief was me sitting in front of him on the floor and holding his legs and praying in the Spirit. We cried and we prayed. He kept an accurate record of every detail and, when he would talk to the specialist (who was a Christian, by the way – how good of God), he would relate these experiences to the doctor. There was nothing which could be done to make it any easier. I really just thought that, at any moment, the miraculous was going to occur and it would all be over and we would go back to our lives. We had Christian television available to us and we watched every man or woman of God who had been used of the Lord to bring healing to others. Every time they prayed for the t.v. audience, we prayed with them. There was one time when a well-known healing evangelist was on and we were both on the floor of the living room praying with him. I thought, for sure, we had his healing that night. I just didn't understand the extent of the fear in my husband. Fear is a terrible thing. It is also a very powerful thing. I had never known my husband to have fear so I was not prepared for it and I didn't realize that it was there as powerfully as it was.

CHAPTER NINE

I DON'T KNOW WHAT TO DO!

O ver the some six months which my husband had been ill, it was his practice to not spend much time in bed because he found it very difficult to sleep lying down. He would always start out in bed but, after two or three hours – maybe not even that long – he would get back up and go in the living room and sit in his lounger. During the days, sitting there, he would study the Word and make notes. He had notebooks full of notes. It was obvious that he really thought that God was going to allow him to preach again. He had those notebooks, Bibles, concordances, and other study helps strategically stationed around his chair within reaching distance. When he would sit in that chair at night, he would pray. He would snooze a little here and there but mostly he prayed. He prayed for hours every night. He prayed for family members, who didn't have a relationship with the Lord – that they would come to know the Lord. He prayed for family members who knew the Lord but had seemed to grow cold toward Jesus – that they would fall back in love with Jesus again. In general, he prayed for everybody. I know he prayed for me. At times when I would wake up in the night, I would hear him in there praying in the Spirit. I simply couldn't stay up with him at night. I had so much on my plate to handle that I just had to get some sleep, but I knew that he prayed all night long.

One night, as we were preparing to take another weekend trip to move some more things, I was awakened by some loud noises and my husband yelling for me. I jumped out of bed and got to him in the living room. He was sobbing very loudly and praying. He was standing, trying to hold himself from falling. He had gone to the kitchen and gotten a big glass of ice water and brought it in and started to set it on the lamp table by his chair. As he leaned down to set the water down, his legs started to give way on him and he began to fall. As he did, the water spilled and was all over his notes, his Bibles, and everything around his chair. He couldn't move without falling. I somehow got a hold of him and got him to another chair in the living room. He was screaming at me to get his notes before they were ruined. I began to hurriedly do what I could to retrieve his papers and books. I took them to lay them out to dry and ran to sop up water from his chair and the carpet. It seemed like a flood from that one glass of water when I was in such a hurry. All the time I was running around doing these things, he was sobbing these great, wracking sobs, and praying more fervently than I had ever heard him pray in his life. He said, "God, if I can't get my healing, then take me Home! I'm no good to my wife, my kids, or my grandkids! I can't make a living and I'm just a drain on my wife! She can't go on like this! She doesn't deserve this! I am responsible for this and I don't want her to have to go on like this! Take me to Heaven, Lord, please – just take me to Heaven! I don't want to go on like this! I don't want to live like this! I want to come Home!" He sobbed these words over and over and over. It seemed like it went on forever. I sat in front of him on the floor holding his legs and praying in the Spirit. After awhile, he began to calm down some. He was absolutely drained of an ability to go on. He was gasping to get his breath. As I prayed, he quieted down and began to breathe with the oxygen a little bit better. We sat quietly like that, with me praying, and with him calming. Some time went by and then he began to pray again, this time quietly and calmly. He told the Lord he was sorry for saying all those things. I don't even think he knew what he had prayed. At any rate, down in the depth of my being, I knew that the fervent prayer which had been coming from him was more fervent than anything I had ever heard --and then I was afraid!

We tried to go back to some sense of normalcy, although what that was at that time, it is hard to determine. I slept for a little while longer and he also did. The next day, I continued preparation to be gone for over the weekend, as well as going on with my normal work. My office was only a few feet away from our apartment and it was my practice to come over to check on him periodically throughout the day. I had been there to fix our lunch and eat lunch with him and, so, a couple of hours after that, I went over to check on him. I couldn't find him. He had carried something out to the car and didn't have enough strength to get back in the house so he was sitting in the car. I helped him back in the house and sat and prayed with him for awhile. I came back over in another hour or so and he didn't look good. He was gasping for breath and couldn't seem to make any of the methods explained by the respiratory therapists to work. I worked with him and prayed with him but nothing seemed to change. I was extremely alarmed. He looked at me with fear and love, all mixed together, and gasped out, "Honey, I think you'd better call 911." I did. The emergency team came and hurriedly began to work on him. As they were getting him on the stretcher, he looked at me and said, "Honey, I'm sorry." That's the last thing he ever said to me.

They got him to the hospital and, when I got there, they were working on him in the emergency room. They did for hours. They had given him something to be able to get a tube down him to help him breathe. He could not respond to me. I began to try to get in touch with my kids. My daughter was about three hours away from me and my son was several states away from me. The next few hours were indescribable. They took him to I.C.U. My daughter, son-in-law, and grandson came to where I was. I prayed like I have never prayed before in my life. I prayed in the Spirit, I prayed with my understanding, I commanded the devil! I sat with my mouth close to his ear and I talked to him. He did not respond to me but I believed that his spirit was still there. About 5:00 in the morning, they lost his vitals and I stood by his bed commanding his spirit back in his body. The nurses and the doctors were giving me a wide berth at that point. They didn't know what they had on their hands. They thought I was just crazy with grief. God sent a spirit-filled lady doctor into the room. She knew what I was talking about and she and I, with my daughter, laid hands on him and prayed. They began to get his vitals again.

Those next few hours were awful, to put it mildly. All of the nurses and doctors kept trying to tell me that if he began to pull out of this now, he wouldn't be the same. My feeling was that if my faith could get him to stay alive, it could get him completely healed. I was crazy with grief and fear! My daughter and I were in and out of the room while my son-in-law stayed in the waiting room with my grandson. Sometime after 10:00 A. M., my daughter was in the room with her daddy and she got down close to his ear and said, "Daddy, if this is all too hard, it's okay if you want to just go on and be with Jesus. Nobody is going to be mad at you. You have fought like I have never seen anyone fight but this thing just is too big, it seems. It's okay, Daddy. I'll take care of Mama. You don't have to worry about her. We'll see that she's okay. I love you, Daddy."

I came back in the room shortly after that and they began to lose his vitals again. Somehow, I knew! I knew that it was over. I couldn't go on trying to keep him here. I knew, in an instant, that this time I couldn't keep praying, keep commanding, keep talking to him. He was on his way to the Savior.

Before long, it was all over. I kept saying, "I can't believe this is happening. It wasn't supposed to be like this." My daughter and son-in-law began to take care of things for me. We had been in contact with my son and he would be with us in several hours. My son is a minister and he wanted to do his daddy's funeral. I wanted him to. The next few days are rather foggy in my mind. That is normal for anyone going through this kind of grief. I know that I am very thankful for my children. They were strong for me when I couldn't be strong. I am not attempting to be dismal or morbid by the telling of these very private things but, instead, I believe there are things which the Lord would like to use from my experience to help others. Thus, I am willing to share them.

From that point of view, I would like to share, with my children's permission, some things from their hearts. The first is a letter that my daughter wrote to her daddy and read at his funeral. This is her memoriam to her father.

Dear Daddy,

As I sit here, I realize this will be my last letter to you. I won't have to seal an envelope. I won't have to lick a stamp. You will never hold this letter in your hands. But you did so enjoy it when I opened up my soul and wrote from my heart. So, my sweet daddy, this letter I write to you.

It's only been a few days since your spirit left your body. But it seems like a lifetime has passed. I miss you so very much

Daddy, you made it. You are finally in the throne room of God. You see the streets of gold. You can hear the angels' voices as they sing their praises. You are seeing loved ones that went before you....your mother and father, Mom's dad, your grandpa and grandma, and even my child, the little spirit we never got to meet. You have already sat with Abraham and talked for hours. You have met Noah, Adam, John, Mary......you have met them all. In an instant, you had all the knowledge of the Lord. You know all the truths, all the keys...you know it all now. What an incredible feeling that must be, Daddy.

Daddy, I am a little frightened. I am a little unsure of the future. Daddy, I miss you.

Daddy, I am so proud of Mom. I know you are too. I know in those final hours you could hear us. I know you saw how Mom did not give up. She stood in the gap for you. I know that you could hear her words of prayer, her words of encouragement to you and her powerful words of faith. You and I know that her undying love and faith is what brought you back to us the first time. And we know that it was also that love and faith that gave you and now all of us the strength to do what we must do. It gave you strength to leave her, and go into God's waiting arms. It gives us strength to carry on, without you in our lives.

Daddy, I want you to know I'm so proud to be your daughter. You fought a battle these last few months that was bigger than you but you fought it with a faith I have never seen the likes of before. Daddy, these last few months, I really got a glimpse of a man I really liked. I know that your emotional state embarrassed you. But, oh Daddy, I will carry the memories of those emotions with me forever. Those emotions made you so tender, so caring, such a joy to be around. Your eyes had such peace about them.

I always dreaded this day, for as long as I can remember. I didn't think I could make it. I thought I would just give up. But, Daddy, I won't give up and I know why. You prayed for me, a lot these last few months. Your prayers will be forever working in my life, giving me strength to face the most difficult things ahead in my life...this being the first. Thank you for praying for me...thank you for never giving up on me.

Daddy, my son will know you. He will see you in Mom; he will see you in me. This isn't the way I had intended the relationship between you two to be, but, as you were the intercessor for us the past five months, we will be the intercessor...the go between... between you and him.

It's time for me to say good-bye now, Daddy. I will never forget you, but you know that. I will take care of Mom, but you know that too. And, Daddy, above all, you know I love you.

Your Little Girl

What a beautiful tribute to her father that my daughter wrote! I wanted it included in this story of mine, because it shows her heart. It also shows the kind of relationship we had in our family – Dad, Mom, Son, and Daughter. Our daughter was very close to her daddy and when he was on the medication, during those last few months, he was extremely emotional. He cried in almost every conversation. It touched her heart deeply. My children and my grandchildren are the legacy that my husband left to me. I am very proud of them.

As I said, my son wanted to do his daddy's funeral. We had a very private, intimate funeral. It was a memorial service, a tribute, and a funeral all rolled into one. My son presented the most beautiful tribute to his father that I have ever heard. There is absolutely nothing that I would have had different. I would like to include here a psalm that my son wrote and read at his daddy's graveside:

A man of God has died today,
Jesus, please take notice.
He spoke the Word to the very end,
He kept his faith in focus.
A man of God has died today,
Please Lord, help me understand.
Your time and purpose for doing this,
For calling home your friend.
A man of God has died today,
His light burned very bright.
God's golf ball has finally come to rest,
He's fought his last good fight.
God, my husband died today,
I don't know what to do.
It wasn't supposed to be like this,
He loved us, me and you.

God, my husband died today,
We've had many wonderful years.
We've loved and hurt, prayed and cried,
I've anointed him with my tears.
God, my daddy died today,
I miss him very much.
It's not us four against the world no more,
I need his loving touch.
A man of God has died today.

That just about summed it up. The four of us – my husband, me, our son, and our daughter – the way we loved one another, no matter what. Nothing could ever change the love. Our son had heard his father call himself, "God's Golfball," many times when he was preaching. My husband had heard another preacher use that phrase many years before and he had told the Lord that he would be ready to move – wherever He wanted him to go.

Ah – my children! How I love them! I love them as the unique, wonderful persons that they both are! And – my how I see my husband in them! My son – in so many ways, is so like my husband.

He has that same kind of "Take Charge!" personality, the same broad shoulders, the same quick mind. When my son was little and he and his daddy were standing side by side, from the back I called them, Big Bear and Little Bear. They walked the same way. I have seen my son exhibit the same teary-eyed tenderness which I saw in my husband through the years.

Oh, my sweet daughter! How like her daddy in so many ways. She has those big, expressive eyes like he had and those deep dimples. She has that same type of compassionate personality like her daddy. My, how she loves to laugh like my husband did. My daughter dearly loves funny things, silly jokes, ridiculous comedy, just like her daddy did. They could tell jokes to each other over the telephone and think nothing of the fact that they were talking long-distance telling jokes. And yet, she is definitely her very own, unique self – her own person.

I am so grateful to the Lord for allowing me to see how wonderful my children have become as adults. I am very proud of them. Their daddy was proud also.

They both did such a wonderful job of "seeing to me" in those first few days. My son had to leave and go home to his family and my daughter helped me begin to face my life and my tasks. She truly carried out that promise to her daddy that she would "take care of Mama."

CHAPTER TEN

IT'S JUST YOU AND ME, JESUS

Needless to say, there have been many kinds of problems, emotions, attitudes, and adjustments but, through it all, the Lord has been ever faithful and I have made many discoveries about myself and about Him. There are no words to describe the emotional trauma of the "splitting apart" of two spirit beings, who have been joined together by God, as my husband and I were. I believe that's what happens at a marriage ceremony. It is much more than just a big show, with beautiful clothes, flowers and music. It's much more than a pronouncement and signature of a preacher or a person licensed to sign such a document. It is a covenant entered into by a man and a woman, as they speak their vows, and I believe that it is holy in the sight of the Lord – these two joined together.

Anyone who has lost a mate has gone through this emotional trauma, these adjustments, this confusion, the stress. I am not unique in what I have been through, but I have understood some rather significant things which, I believe, will help others.

The absolute first thing I had to face – remember I'm talking about discoveries I made, not problems – was that I wanted answers from the Lord regarding my husband's death. I pretty much had dealt with the fact of why he got sick. Contrary to the way I would have believed years ago, I did not believe that God made him sick. I did not believe that God was trying to teach him something. I did not believe that the Lord was angry at him for leaving the ministry, for making unwise choices, for making mistakes. If that were the case, the Lord would be angry at the entire population of the Church. I had already concluded, in my mind, based on what I had discovered about the grace of God, that God loves us, His children, very much. All His anger at sin and disobedience was poured out on Jesus on the cross. We, as His children, are forgiven for our sins – past, present, and future sins. I heard my husband say many times, when he was preaching, "Which of your sins was future when Jesus died on the cross?" Of course, the answer to that is, "All of them." We weren't even born yet. In other words, we – the Church – aren't being punished for sin. That was poured out on Jesus. We either believe that or we do not.

Therefore, I pretty well understood that this physical problem had not come from God and that, for some reason, we had not gotten his healing. I wanted to know why we had not gotten his healing. In the midst of my misery, grief, confusion, and uncertainty about the future, the Lord comforted me with a peace that truly was unexplainable to natural, human reasoning. I found myself trusting Him as never before in my life. I have always talked with the Lord in an intimate way – not in a religious way – sharing my innermost thoughts and concerns with Him. I found myself asking Him the question, "Why?" over and over again. I felt so alone, in the natural sense, but, at the same time, I have never been so aware of the presence of the Lord. I began to realize that I had completely suppressed, deep within the recesses of my being, the experience which had occurred several hours before taking my husband to the hospital. I had literally buried it. The Lord brought it to my remembrance and began to show me that my husband had prayed, from the center of his being, the most fervent prayer ever prayed in his life.

I had known, from the days in which I learned about praying for others, when I prayed for my daughter, that the Lord would not violate the human will. I learned, through that experience, that God wants us to pray for others in accordance with His will. As we ask Him, He will enter into the affairs of man, but that His way is to speak, urge, woo, teach, call, draw, etc. and the individual must respond to the Lord. We do not indiscriminately pray for God to just save or heal everybody in the world. We pray for Him to enter into their affairs and draw them to Him. We don't have to beg God to do those wonderful things, which He delights in doing for His children, whom He loves. He is always ready to save, heal, and meet needs. That is His will. However, the human will is very strong. We have all heard it spoken, "She just lost her will to live." I was praying for my husband's healing but his true, honest, heartfelt desire was expressed on that night when he "spent" himself in praying with tears and fervency. I had to face that. It was not easy. I felt like he had deserted me. I felt like he had again chosen the Lord over me. I felt very alone. It was at that deepest, loneliest time that, through my tears, I cried out, "It's just You and me, Jesus!"

As I reflected back on the last several months, I realized that there had been little signs along the way that he was having difficulty with this disease beyond his capabilities. The Lord helped me see that many, many times, it was me doing the praying and believing. The symptoms were often more than his endurance could handle. Put that together with his embarrassment over being in this condition, his guilt that he was responsible for this huge load being on me, and the fear that he was not used to dealing with, and it was all just bigger than him. He just wanted out of that body. He wanted to worship the Lord unhindered. He wanted freedom from the flesh. I also believe that he saw passing through death as the way to give me a life again, rather than caring for an invalid, while he tried to get his healing.

These things were not easy to deal with in my mind, but I had decided that I wanted "real" answers, not just ones to soothe me. There was no doubt in my mind that my husband loved me. I really didn't know how on earth I was going to go on without him. I truly didn't know what to do, but neither did I want to explain things to myself in false platitudes and fake statements which people adopt at times of the death of a loved one. We've all heard them – "He's just in a better place now." "He's not suffering anymore." "The Lord needed him in heaven." I was determined that I was going to face reality, based on the Word of God, and the awareness deep within me of what I knew about the nature of God, and the way He had always spoken to my heart to give me comfort, revelation, and guidance. I said some very bold things to the Lord in those days and I opened myself to Him for Him to speak some very bold things to me. I made up my mind that I didn't want to live another day of my life just going through life as the rest of the world does. The world eats, sleeps, works, buys, launders, bathes, cleans, etc. I am a child of the Most High God. I want my life to accomplish something from here on out. I had wasted time. Regardless of all that I had not done up to then, I wanted to be available to Him for the rest of my life. I told the Lord, "I yield the right-of-way to you. It's just You and me, Jesus."

I determined that I wanted answers from the Lord about what to do with the rest of my life more than I wanted anything else in life. Absolutely nothing else mattered to me except to know what God wanted. I talked to Him, I sang to Him, I worshipped Him with my understanding and in other tongues. I read His Word with a new zeal. I had always loved the Word of God but it was as though it had become new and alive all over again to me. I had lots of problems in the financial realm and I simply did not know what to do. It would be great if I could say that all of those problems just vanished away as I spent time with the Lord. I can't say that! I wasn't sure what I was supposed to do with my life from that point on. My husband and I had talked many times in the six months before his death about going back into the ministry again. Deep in my heart, I knew that's what I really wanted; but there seemed to be absolutely no way that I could fathom that it could take place. I remember lying on my face before the Lord, praying, and telling the Lord that I would serve Him in any capacity at all. It didn't matter what it was that He wanted me to do, I would do it. I was honest with Him. Why try to fool God? I told Him that I would love to teach His Word again and I asked Him if He would allow me to do that. I told Him that, if He wanted me to, though, I would be one of those "pray-ers" – the ones He trusts to do the praying, on their faces before Him. I told Him that I was willing to do that the rest of my life, if that's what He wanted. I have, for a long time, been aware of the value of real prayer for others and I believe some of the greatest Christians are not necessarily the ones out in front being vocal for the Lord, but the ones nobody ever sees, on their faces before Him, hour after hour. I meant it, with all my heart. I wanted what He wanted. The Lord knew my heart. It's the heart attitude that matters.

I sat by myself, on several occasions, with the communion elements, prepared by me, for just me alone. That may be surprising to some who have never done that, but it was extremely meaningful to me to sit before the Lord alone and sing to Him, and read what He had said at the "Last Supper," and tell Him how much I loved Him. "It's just You and me, Jesus."

I had some other things to face up to!

CHAPTER ELEVEN

I ONLY KNEW HOW TO BE MARRIED

As often is the case with the Lord, the more I spent time with Him, worshipping Him, seeking answers to the "Where do I go from here?" questions, He began to show me things which opened up whole new avenues of thinking for me. Let me make it clear that He did not rebuke me or "take me to the woodshed." He began to lovingly show me things in answer to my questions. The Bible says, in the book of James, that if we lack wisdom, we may ask of God and He will give it liberally to us and He won't get mad at us for asking. (My version!) I began to discover more about Him and I also began to discover some things about myself and the way I had always been – and those things I didn't like. I had told the Lord that I was through playing games in life. I wanted to be real. I wanted to be transparent. I didn't want to live a life, looking one way but being a different way on the inside. I didn't want to ever be a fake or be hypocritical. The Lord began to open me up and show me some things in my attitude about Him.

This was very difficult for me, because He began to deal with me in the core of my being, in the realm of my life which had been the dearest thing to me – my marriage. It hurt to even think about it. I only knew how to be married. I didn't think of myself as a single person. I remember distinctly going to the grocery store the first time after my husband died. It was a horrible experience. I didn't know what to buy. That may sound strange but I am absolutely truthful. For so many years, I had centered in on what my husband liked to eat that I honestly didn't know what to buy. I left the store in tears, not buying anything, because I felt so lost.

I am not talking about just the changing of a lifestyle. Many people face that daily. It went much deeper than that for me. I am not talking about the natural patterns of life that people go through as things change in life. I am talking about the very essence of one's attitude, as a Christian, toward one's mate.

The Lord has shown it to me this way. From the day we met, my man had been first with me. Nothing else in life mattered to me as much as my man and, subsequently, my marriage. I had followed my husband, each step of the way, in the things of God. Please don't misunderstand. I did love God, but to be brutally honest with myself, I have had to admit that my husband had first place in my heart. I do not mean to imply that he dominated me to the point that I was his slave, or that I was afraid to open my mouth. None of that was the case. In fact, he was not to blame for my attitudes. We can never blame others, no matter how much we want to, for the attitudes we have within ourselves. Let me say it this way. If there was a throne in my heart, my husband would have been on that throne, not the Lord. We are responsible, each one of us, for whom we allow to sit on the throne in our hearts. These things I am saying here are things I did not know before. If anyone had suggested that this was the case, I would have denied it.

With the Lord's guidance, I began to think back through the years and I could see that always my first and foremost question, attitude, and decision was based on how it would affect my husband, what my husband would think about it, and what he would say or do. From the very beginning of my walk with the Lord, after my husband had come to the Lord, everything in the spiritual realm was always judged, within me, on the basis of my husband's thinking. It was already that way for me in the natural realm and I just seemed to flow into that way of thinking in the spiritual realm. The strong teaching on submission, along the way, both in the evangelical, fundamental, nondenominational world as well as the charismatic world only strengthened this attitude in me.

After we met and got engaged and my husband was sent overseas in the military for thirteen months, we decided between ourselves that we never wanted to be apart again. Many people say that but we actually meant it and lived that way. We didn't do things separately. We really were each other's best friend. We really enjoyed each other's company. We understood each other. We would rather be with each other than with anyone else.

The Word of God compares the relationship between husband and wife to the relationship between Christ and the church in Ephesians 5. The husband is to love the wife as Christ loves the church and gave Himself for it. When a husband pours out devotion, attention, care, romance, tenderness, and all the things that a woman desires, the woman responds to him because God made the woman to be a responder. However, He never meant for the wife to worship the husband instead of the Lord. Now I never would have thought that I worshipped my husband. But I know in my heart that if it ever came right down to it as to whether I was going to follow the Lord or follow my husband, if there was conflict, I would have followed my husband. In fact I did! I began to see that I had somehow seen my marriage relationship as the most important thing in my life, instead of the Lord and my relationship with Him. As I looked back, I thought of the times when I could have taken a stand, quietly and lovingly, and told my husband that I was going to follow the Lord and what He wanted – that I would continue to pray for him that he would walk close to the Lord also. I recognized that the reason that I had never been brave enough to do that was the terrible fear of being without my husband. I was more afraid of being without him than I was in love with the Lord. That has been a very hard thing for me to admit and to deal with. I don't mean that I was afraid of not being able to make it economically in the world. I am capable of making a living. I mean that the very thought of my husband and me being apart was too much for me to bear.

When we closed the church, I knew that my husband was going down the wrong path. I had taught many, many women how to pray for their families and many of those women had seen success and their families restored. I knew how to pray. I knew what it took. I also knew that my husband loved me; however, there was a gripping fear that if I took the kind of stand that it would take, it could put him in an awkward circumstance, and I might find myself for a period of time without him. I was not willing to risk that.

I also began to realize that, deep within myself, I knew that I was not willing to do what I had taught others to do. In my eyes, that made me a hypocrite. I faced up to the fact that the knowledge of what I thought about myself had, in many ways, hindered me since that dark night on that sofa in the living room when I made my choice to follow my husband.

One day, as I wept and prayed before the Lord concerning these things, the Lord spoke to my heart and revealed to me that this very thing was what Jesus was talking about in Matthew 16:24 – 25. "Then Jesus said to His disciples, 'If anyone wishes to come after Me, let him deny himself, and take up his cross, and follow Me, for whoever wishes to save his life shall lose it; but whoever loses his life for My sake shall find it."(NASB) The Lord told me that I should read verse 25 like this for me, "For whoever wishes to save his marriage shall lose it; but whoever loses his marriage for My sake shall find it." Please understand that I am not trying to change the Word of God or add anything to it. This is what I want you to see. No one should be more dear and precious to you than your Jesus. No one should sit on the throne of your heart but your Jesus. As wonderful a relationship as marriage is, your mate did not die for your sins. It is not wise to love someone more than your Jesus. What do I mean? Did God take my husband from me to show me that He did not have first place in my life? No! No! A thousand times "No!" Because I operated in fear – fear of losing my loved one – I did not trust the Lord and stand strong in faith as I knew to do. I was afraid. The Lord showed me – and this was very hard – that if I had done what I had taught others to do, our lives would have been very different, and my husband might be with me now.

Whatever we seek to "save" and hold dear to us, more precious to us than our Savior, we risk losing. By the same token, when we place that precious person in the Lord's hands and <u>trust</u> Him to take care of the situation while we hold tight to the Lord – with Him first in our lives – He can always be trusted.

So, my friend, I had to come to grips with some very hard facts if I wanted to be extremely honest with the Lord. I only knew how to be married – but I wasn't married anymore. I only knew how to be part of a couple – but the Lord was revealing to me that He had always wanted to be my "All in All." We sing songs and choruses such as, "He's All I Need," but now He was saying to me that those had only been words to me before. He wanted to make it real to me. He wanted to teach me that He truly was "All" I need. My Jesus was revealing to me that He would see to my every need. He would take care of me. He would protect me. He would be my Companion, my Friend, my Confidante, my Helper, my Partner, my Teacher. The Lord showed me that I was not the only Christian who had missed this important part of this wonderful, supernatural life which the Lord has for us. He revealed to me that very few Christians really live on this earth the way the Lord has provided for them to live – because to live that way requires living "by grace through faith."

CHAPTER TWELVE

I AM MY BELOVED'S
AND HE IS MINE

I would like to tell you that, with the understanding of these things that God was showing me, came solutions to all my problems and that they all just vanished. That, however, is not true. What is true, though, is that the more intimate I became with the Lord in daily worship, prayer, and study, the more convinced I became that He would show me, "the way."

I have come to believe that most Christians do not know the first thing about being intimate with the Lord and, yet, it is at the heart of what God intended for us. I had been a pray-er for years. I knew about the power of prayer for others. I also have been a student of the Word for most of my adult Christian life. Most Christians are familiar with prayer, to some extent and have brought a few petitions to the Lord. Also, most have read the Bible, to some degree. However, I am talking about something which goes far beyond these familiarities. People talk about Jesus being their personal Savior, and they talk about having a personal relationship with the Lord; however, most of the time they mean that when they die, they will go to heaven because they believe that He is the Son of God. That, of course, is the truth. But – oh, there is so much more! He desires to intimately be a part of our lives in every way.

I began to look forward with expectancy to each day and the

time I would spend with Him. I found that my times of prayer were not just me talking with repeated phrases from the Word, as they used to be. There was a time, years ago, when all I knew to do was either read the Word, quote the Word to Him regarding any specific thing I was asking Him to do for me, or confessing sin. I began to find that, in the midst of a very difficult situation, with all kinds of problems and very few solutions, I was experiencing a joy, which was not based on circumstances and was not based on the things of this world. This joy was coming from the inside of me and seemed to be what I had read about in the epistles of the New Testament. This was the joy, which was to be at the very heart of the Christian's life. This is the joy, which the apostles experienced even though they were being imprisoned and their circumstances were dreadful. This Jesus, who had been raised from the dead, was living His life now on the inside of them and they were intimately acquainted with Him every hour of every day. He was the source of the joy. This was indeed a personal relationship with a wonderful Companion, Friend, Helper, Partner, and Teacher.

This intimacy is new every morning, fresh every day, fulfilling and alive. I found that before I even opened my eyes in the morning, I wanted to say, "Good Morning," to my Lord. I didn't <u>have</u> to pray, or have a quiet time. I couldn't wait to pray. I wanted to thank Him for another day to be with Him. I wanted to thank Him for keeping watch over me while I slept. I wanted to say things like King David had said to Him in the Psalms. I wanted to sing little songs to Him, which would probably have sounded silly to anyone else, but I had the distinct impression that He loved to hear them. Sometimes they were little rhymes; other times it was just me - talking to Him to the tune of a song I already knew. Often I would just say to Him all the things He is to me – like Redeemer, Lord, Friend, etc. – only in the form of a song.

As I spent time with Him, I discussed with Him what I should do about all these problems which needed solutions, but my motivation for spending time with Him was not to get answers to problems, as it had often been in the past. I discussed my feelings about things. I told Him how much I missed my husband. I explained to Him how I felt – I didn't know where I really fit with people anymore. I was so used to not having to give an explanation of why I say everything I say on a daily basis. Everyone who has been married knows what I mean. You just talk. You don't preface every word you say with why you feel that way, etc., because your mate already knows. I missed that desperately. I told Him so.

I told Him how beautiful I thought His creation is – the colors of the flowers, etc. I told Him what a glorious creation the human body was. I thanked Him for my mind, my will, and my emotions. I asked Him to fill those areas of my life with more of Himself.

I told Him what I needed and I asked Him to supply those things. One day, when I was praying like this, I had been meditating on Philippians 4:19 and praying about some financial needs. He spoke to my heart and said, "Where's your husband?" I replied, "He's in heaven with You, Lord." He again asked, "Where's your husband?" I started to answer Him the same way and said, "Lord, he's with You in.........GLORY." Phil. 4:19 (NASB) says, "And my God shall supply all your needs according to His riches in glory in Christ Jesus." He asked, "Do you think he has any needs in glory?" I answered, "Of course not." He then said to me, "It's the same riches in the same glory that that verse in Philippians is talking about. Your needs are met by that riches in that glory."

The more I became intimate with the Lord, the more I began to understand spiritual things, which had been hard to understand before. I began to comprehend the meaning of verses in the New Testament which had always been vague to me or had seemed to be too super-spiritual for real people to get a hold of and to walk in. For instance, I began to understand "abiding," in Him, "being content with such as you have," "walking in the spirit." These are all wonderful Bible truths which I myself have taught but I began to understand in reality what they mean – not just what they mean mentally, through word studies, or in theory.

I began to have insight into the power and the love which the early Christians experienced in their lives and which caused them to be able to live and die in victory and glory. I began to experience a love affair with Jesus, which, I believe was the essence of the relationship those men and women had with the Son of God. And it was real! I began to experience a moment by moment, hour by hour, day by day walk with complete awareness that He is in me, guiding me, comforting me, teaching me. In other words, I began to experience what I had taught for years was possible in a relationship with the Lord, and had thought I understood. It is truly the "personal relationship with the Lord," that we have all been talking to people about for years and so few of us have walked in ourselves. In this "personal relationship with the Lord," there is no other human being in it with you – no husband, no wife, no children, no parents, no grandparents, no brothers or sisters. Only you and Him! Only your Beloved and you! The relationships in the human realm are all secondary to the relationship with your Lord.

You see, these are all truths that I thought I knew. These are truths, which I would have been quick, like most other believers, to say I believed with all my heart. These are truths, which I thought were deeply rooted in me. But, when it came down to this very difficult crisis in my life, I had to face up to whether they were really real to me or not.

I have heard single women and men say for years that they just knew that it would be easier for them to live the Christian life if they just had someone to share their lives with. I have found that to be untrue. Jesus makes me complete. I had thought, for years, that my husband and I completed each other – that each one, without the other, was not complete. I had heard that taught and I embraced that and taught it also. We might have complemented each other but we did not complete each other. Col. 2:10 says that, "and in Him, you have been made complete...." (NASB) Every person I know, who has asked the Lord for a mate, and received the perfect one for him or her, has been honest with the Lord and said that they were lonely and wanted to share life with someone. That someone cannot be your completeness, or help you "live for the Lord." You are complete in Him.

Let me say, along these lines, also, that to look to any other individual, instead of the Lord, to be the one to "take care of you," is to go down a road that leads to problems. Every believer is complete in Him. Every believer can look to Him for truly everything in life.

As I read through the New Testament and the Psalms over and over again, in every translation or version that I could get my hands on, I really found myself being transformed. I was familiar with "the renewing of the mind." I understood that the New Testament teaches that when we are born again, our spirits are no longer dead but made alive unto God but our minds must be renewed. A person must retrain, or reprogram his mind to see things like God sees them. I understood that this process of the renewing of the mind takes place as one takes in the Word of God and begins to "not think like the world," and, instead, "think like Jesus." I still believe that! However, as I began to read the New Testament and put myself into the crowd listening to Jesus preach, I saw that I had to "really" listen to Him. I had to be the one who felt His touch as my body was healed. I had to be the one whose daughter was raised from the dead. I had to be the one who received my sight, my hearing, my cleansing from leprosy. I had to be one in that crowd eating until I was full from a few loaves and fishes. Then – I began to see what I hadn't seen before! We must each personally allow the Son of God to transform us by believing what He said in His Word deep within us. We must believe that it is true for us – not just true for the world "out there" in some vague, mystical sense – but for us individually. I must believe what He said applies to me, because He is living in me. The Spirit of Jesus – the Person! His Word, what He said, is wonderful. I love it! I live by it. It is in me. But He, Jesus, the Person, is capable of doing the same thing today in my life, as He did in those I read about. Salvation is not just a ticket to heaven – escaping hell. Yes, it is that; but it is so much more. Let me explain what the Lord made real to me.

I had to be there when He was crucified – when my sins were borne by Him. I had to hear him cry, "It is finished!" I had to watch while they took Him down and carried Him away to the tomb. I had to be there when the disciples said, "He's not there; He's risen!" I had to be there when He appeared to all of them and said, "Touch Me; I'm not a ghost." I had to watch while He stood on that Israeli hillside and began to rise toward heaven.

The power and reality of what those first believers experienced was what carried them to the upper room to wait for the baptism in the Holy Spirit. That love and forgiveness is what enabled Peter to preach to all those people that day without fear. He, himself, had been forgiven, even though he had personally betrayed the Lord, and he had watched Him as He rose toward heaven. It was real to him. That glorious reality is what gave Stephen the devotion to stand there and say what He'd heard the Lord say about His killers. It's what drew him to look into heaven and see Jesus. Saul, on the road to Damascus, when the blinding light came from heaven, remembered holding the coats while the people stoned Stephen. He remembered hearing what Stephen said. His salvation, baptism, baptism in the Holy Spirit and healing was not just a ticket to heaven. It was not just forgiveness of all his sins. It was much more. It was truly a PERSONAL relationship with the One who had spoken the world into existence.

I began to think about all those people in the cities and villages that began to hear and respond to the gospel where all the apostles, deacons, pastors, prophets, teachers, and disciples working miracles and healing people traveled. I began to see myself as one of those new Christians in Ephesus, or Colosse, or Philippi. I saw myself as one who had been an idol-worshipper, a person in sin and ignorance. I saw myself as a Hebrew, who thought, because of my birth, I was okay with God.

There was no daily repetition of Scripture in their lives to transform them. They didn't even have a Bible. They turned from darkness to light and the Son of God transformed them as they got to know Him intimately and believed His promises. I saw that there is a difference between repeating the Scriptures to try to become something or someone and believing that He has already done in me what He said He would do. I saw, as I put myself into their lives, which is so beautifully recorded for us in the Scriptures, that they believed the message they heard about Him. They stopped going one way and started going another way. That, after all, is what repentance is. Then they began to trust Him, based on the stories, which they were told. They were told what He had said that He would do for them. They simply believed Him. They began to talk with Him, themselves, and trust Him on an individual basis. The preachers, like the Apostle Paul, would come their way and tell them more about what He had revealed. They believed it and acted upon it. Great believers like Paul, Peter, John and James would write them letters and tell them more about what God was like and how they were to conduct themselves now that they belonged to His family, not to get God to love them more but because He loved them so much and they could act just like Him because He had already made them like Him on the inside.

Paul told them about the "mystery," the church, hidden before that time, and who they really were now "In Christ." Peter told them about being an "eyewitness." John explained "love" to them. James taught them about "believing and doing." Of course, each of these men of God told them much more but the important thing to realize is that they were being told about God and about who they now were IN CHRIST and they believed it and acted upon it.

As I read the New Testament from this kind of perspective, I began to see that it's not hard to trust Someone, Whom you have gotten to know so well. Those Christians of that first century changed the world with their preaching, teaching, and healing, not because they had a good program, but because they got to know a Person. From reading the Acts of the Apostles, it doesn't appear that Peter and the others went through a real strain to know if they really could go out and get people healed. They just believed the One whom they had gotten to know so intimately.

Again, I must say that this "personal relationship with the Lord," which we have preached so much for so many years, has been really a mystery to most of us. What we have meant is "ticket to heaven." However, my friend, His plan has always been for you and me to have an intimate relationship with Him. Most people, I have discovered, are embarrassed when you talk about intimacy with the Lord. You can say, "devotions," "quiet time," "prayer time," but when you say, "intimacy," it seems to conjure up pictures, brings on confusion, doesn't seem real religious, and in general is not understood.

Let's talk about intimacy. The title of this Chapter, "I Am My Beloved's and He is Mine," is taken from the Song of Solomon. Most people really don't read that book in the Bible much because it seems to be so sensual and has so much to say about the bride and the bridegroom. I have heard it said that it doesn't seem to be real spiritual. I believe that it is a picture of the relationship between each believer and the Lord, and then the believers, corporately, and the Lord. In the New Testament, Paul talks about the marriage relationship in the book of Ephesians as a picture of the relationship between the church and the Lord. Because that has been so tough to handle, much has been made of the natural things, which were said and doctrines have been preached which have put people in bondage. The whole point of intimacy with the Lord was missed.

The truth of the matter is that no matter how much we read the Bible, go to church, go to Bible studies, read Christian books, etc., none of these things is a substitute for getting to really <u>know</u> the Lord. The way you get to know Him is by spending time with Him. I am very much aware of how much our lives are governed by our watches and clocks but you must spend time with someone to really get to know the individual. Husbands and wives, who do not spend time together and really talk to one another, have a communication problem when crisis comes. Many of them end in divorce. It won't do to know <u>about</u> Him. I was saved and I knew about Him for years. I could quote Scripture; I taught the Bible; I had Bible knowledge; I even knew a considerable amount about prayer and had experienced some success in getting prayers answered. I knew the names of great men and women of the faith. I had considerable knowledge about the great revivals of the church. But – I'm talking about <u>KNOWING HIM</u>.

My husband and I knew each other so well that we could team teach very comfortably. We each knew what kind of thing the other would say. We trusted each other so completely in this that we did not fear at all that the other one would do or say something to make us look bad. We knew how each other felt and we could count on each other always acting in a certain way. We knew each other.

That's what I have discovered that God wants for each of us in our relationship with Him. He wants us to know Him so well that we will always know what to expect from Him. No matter what life presents us, we can know what He will do. No matter what comes our way, we can be certain of what to expect – not because we have memorized so many scripture verses – but because we are so intimate with Him and we know Him so well, we are sure of Him. That's what the early Christians experienced. Please don't misunderstand. It's good to have the Word of God committed to memory. I am forever grateful for the Word, which is in me. But I have learned to say, with the Apostle Paul, "To know Him, and the power of His resurrection." (Phil. 3:10)

CHAPTER THIRTEEN

JESUS IN ME

A s far back as I can remember, I have heard about Jesus coming into your inner man. I remember the pictures from Sunday School of Jesus standing at a door, knocking. The door was supposed to represent the inside of an individual and I can't ever remember not knowing that Jesus would come in if you would invite Him. In the evangelical circles which make up a large portion of Christianity, Jesus coming into the believer is fairly well accepted as a description of the born again experience. In the more liturgical portions of Christianity, which really do not consider themselves as evangelical, it is still commonly understood that Jesus comes in. I remember the days of the Charismatic Renewal, mixing with people of denominations that I, heretofore, had not even believed were saved. It was quite an eye-opening experience to realize that perhaps they had a different idea than I did about many things but they believed that, at some point, Jesus had come into them.

Through the years, as I had studied the Word, I had come to believe that at the moment that a person believes, in his heart, and confesses with his mouth, as it says in Rom. 10:9-10, he is made new on the inside. I believe that, at that very moment, many things happen – forgiveness of sin, etc., but one of the things that happens is that the Spirit of Christ takes up residence in you. (Rom 8:9) One cannot tell, from looking at your flesh, that anything has changed. Your hair is still the same; your eyes are still the same; your skin is still the same; in other words, you are changed on the inside – not the outside.

I personally believe, through the study of the Word, that the baptism in the Holy Spirit is a separate experience from the new birth. I believe that the book of Acts makes this clear. However, I believe also that many times that experience can occur so closely to the new birth that it almost seems like it is all one experience. Let me say, also, that I believe there are many, many people who are born again but who have never experienced the baptism of the Holy Spirit. That does not make them any less Christians. The Bible criteria for being born again is believing with the heart and confessing with the mouth. I believe, however, that no one is ever baptized in the Holy Spirit unless they are born again.

Having said all of that, let me say now that I have come to believe that a great percentage of Christians never experience, now, in this life, many of the benefits of the new birth – Jesus in us. Victory in the Christian life, victory over the flesh, walking in the spirit is all very much misunderstood. I have said in previous chapters that my husband and I searched for years for the answer. Each time that we would dig a little deeper and experience something new in God, we would expect it to be the key to living the Christian life. All the time, victory over the flesh, walking in the spirit was right there in the new birth – Jesus in us.

I can remember years ago reading my Bible, especially the New Testament, and thinking, "This is impossible! I can't do this! I can't be this loving, this pure, this holy, this selfless, this kind, etc.! Why does God make it so hard?" For years and years, I thought that. Please understand – I really thought it would be wonderful if I could be like Jesus. I would read the Gospels and I really wanted with all my heart to act like He acted. I would read the Epistles and read about the wonderful God-kind-of-love that should have been operating in my life. I wanted to be like that. I wanted to act like Jesus, talk like Jesus, think like Jesus! I tried to! I would read the Word and study the Word. I would become convinced that I was supposed to be able to be like Jesus so I would make up my mind that I was going to change me. I was going to change the way I thought, talked, acted, etc. I <u>would</u> walk in love toward everyone, especially the unlovely. I would do it! As I understood it, it was all up to me, the renewing of my mind. I would always fail and, then, of course, I would feel guilty.

If it was a merry-go-round for me, I knew it was much, much rougher on my husband. Why do I say that? Because we were different personalities! I did a two-tape-series teaching years ago, when our church was going very well, called, "Why Opposites Attract, and How to Live With Them." I had not read any psychological books – the Lord just gave me the understanding as I prayed one day. I have since discovered that there are books, now on the market with some of that which the Lord gave to me, to help people understand personality types. My husband and I were opposites. I called him a Type A and me a Type B. I was more of a quiet-type person; he was not. I could just flow with a situation, which might be a little uncomfortable; he could not seem to do that. He would always, it seemed, <u>have</u> to speak his mind, and, it seemed, lock horns with someone. It appeared to me that if he would just be quiet, we would have less problems. He felt like I needed to speak up more instead of being quiet when he felt like something needed to be addressed. I would always rather avoid confrontation; he would rather meet it head on. I would rather be in the background than the limelight; he loved the limelight. I was more the follower; he was the leader. You see, we were certainly opposites! All of these kinds of things in his personality were strong, forceful characteristics which, when trained by the flesh for years and years, were deeply ingrained in him. My personality traits were deeply ingrained in me also, but, by the very nature of my personality, mine were not as strong. You see, we were both strong-willed but he was more vocal and outward with his opinions, ideas, etc. Mine were more inward.

He, being the type of person that he was, as well as a perfectionist, could see the way the Christian life was supposed to be, and he would make up his mind to live it that way. He would embark on it the way he did everything else. He would jump in with both feet and figured if anybody could do it, he could. He often had the attitude through life that if God had something He needed to get done and couldn't get anybody else to do it, he would do it. He even prayed that way. As I said in an earlier chapter, he called himself, "God's Golfball." Therefore, his attitude was, "I can do this." "I will do this." "I will do this because I want to."

I now know that for what it is. I attempted to do it also but because of his personality, the "take-off" was much splashier and the "landing" was much harder and was much more dramatic. I now know that this is trying to attain a spiritual result with the flesh. Let me say this as simply as I know how. In our flesh – our physical body, our mind, our will, our emotions – we cannot live the Christian life! It is impossible! Jesus said, "Apart from me, you can do nothing." (John 15:5 NASB) Our wonderful Savior not only took our sin to the cross for us and paid the price that we could not pay, but after He had risen from the dead, and had gone to the Father, He came back to live in us – to do what we cannot do (the Spirit of Christ). I personally believe that this is the most misunderstood thing in the Christian life.

I have discovered, and am daily discovering, that, moment by moment, I must rely on Jesus in me for absolutely everything. I can do nothing in myself. There are, I believe, two opposite views, which are truly misconceptions in this realm. Let's discuss these two views in order to see the truth.

There is the view that I will call, "The Lowly Worm." That view is that I am just an old sinner, saved by grace. Yes, I was saved by grace, but I was bad and, in order to keep myself in line and not think of myself too highly, I must remember constantly how bad I was. I never know when I might get out of line again. I'm just like I was before I was saved except that now I'm on my way to heaven. I have to keep asking for forgiveness because there's probably stuff that I don't even know that I do wrong all the time. God will always prod me and poke me and, one of these days, I will finally make it to heaven. I am not worth much on this earth; I'm just "an old sinner, saved by grace."

The other view I will call the "I Can," view. This view says that the Lord has made me new on the inside and now I am just like Him. Whatever He did, I can do. He did it. I can do it. There is nothing that I cannot do. I am capable. I am strong. In fact, I am perfect now. I don't even sin anymore. I am smart. In fact, I have the mind of Christ. Therefore, what I say is always right and perfect. Nothing can stand in my way. In fact, I deserve everything good to come to me. I am on my way. I am full of ability and strength. I am wonderful. I can!

There is truth in both of these views – but now let me say what I have discovered to be the truth.

Yes, I was a sinner. I was a descendant of Adam and, because of that, I was a sinner. I could not save myself, and – yes, I was bad! But Jesus took my sin. All the wrath of God for my sin was poured out on Jesus. Therefore, all my sins – past, present, and future – are forgiven. I have received Jesus as my Savior and, therefore, forgiveness. The sin question for me is settled. My performance – good or bad – is no longer an issue. God loves me and has accepted me in His family. That, in itself, motivates me to not want to sin; but, if I do, I just tell Him that I wish I hadn't and that I'm so glad I am forgiven. I am not under any misconceptions about my wrongdoing – my sin – but I just see it for what it is and, then recognizing who I am in Christ and what He has done for me, I go on. I express my gratitude to Him for forgiveness and my worship of Him takes on more meaning each new day. Yes, I am strong but my strength *IS IN THE LORD*. Everything good in me is not because of me but *BECAUSE OF THE LORD*.

Somewhere, deep in me, Jesus has come to dwell. God made my spirit new and He, in the Person of the Holy Spirit (the Spirit of Christ) has come to live in my new spirit. My new spirit is perfect and pure, just like Him. He isn't just guiding me from up in heaven somewhere. He is here with me, in me. He loves me so much and He has come to teach me, to help me, to comfort me, to guide me, to protect me. He knows what it's like to live in flesh on this earth. He did it and He didn't sin once. He knows my weaknesses. He also knows that I love Him. He knows that I want to do good but my flesh is weak. He's told me that I can depend on Him and He will help me.

Therefore, I recognize that it is Jesus in me who does good. He gave me a new spirit and then He came to live in that new spirit. It is Jesus who loves through me, if I will trust Him. It is Jesus who lives this Christian life through me, if I will trust Him. If I try to live this life with my own willpower, my own mental ability, my own emotional strength, I will fall flat on my face because that is my flesh. The works of the flesh! The Christian life can only be lived with His strength, His power, His love. I am deeply aware that I could not save my soul. I had to receive salvation by grace through faith. (Eph. 2:8) I must live this life of grace the same way I received salvation – by faith.

Essentially, it's this way! "I recognize, Lord, that I cannot do this. I ask you to do it, please." My body, my mind, my will, and my emotions, as well as my heart, all play a part of the total "Me" and those parts are influenced both by the new spirit – where Jesus lives – on the inside of me and by the physical world around me. My body, with the mind, will, and emotions can be "renewed" or reprogrammed, and I have been involved in doing that for years and years. However, if I try to live the Christian life – all that love, all that good, all that beautiful, wonderful, holy way of living which is the way Jesus lived – by the renewed mind, will, emotions, etc., I am attempting to gain a spiritual result from a fleshly action. I will fall flat on my face – depending on my own ability. I did that for years! So did my husband! It is so simple – this life of grace - yet so misunderstood. Do you see why I said that I believe this is the most misunderstood thing in the Christian life?

As I now see it, there is no difference in living this life of grace through the power of the risen Christ, who dwells within, and in doing tremendous miracles for the Lord. When Peter and John started to go into the temple for their daily prayer meeting in Acts 3, they were asked by a crippled man for money. They told him, essentially, that they didn't have any but that they had something better. They lifted him to his feet and told him to "Walk, in Jesus' name." He did! This notable miracle caused quite a stir and one of the things Peter told them was, (in my words) "Why are you looking at us as though this was our power or holiness that did this? This miracle was done by the name of Jesus, and faith in that name."

Peter's flesh, or John's flesh, did not perform this miracle. It was Jesus performing the miracle. Peter and John could not take pride in what they had done. They hadn't done anything! They were only believing in the words which Jesus had spoken to them. They believed that He had come to dwell in them. He had the power.

They just believed. The Son of God had come to dwell in them. They had seen Him heal people when he walked in a physical body with them from village to village. He had told them that He would come to be in them. He had told them to just go do what He did. They believed. They couldn't get prideful or big-headed over the miracle. They knew that, in their flesh, they couldn't do anything like this. It was Jesus in them.

Living the Christian life is the same way. It is a life of faith. Because the word, "faith," has been a little misunderstood here and there, let's substitute the word, "trust." Because I believe that He has come to live in me, His power and His love are available to me. However, I must recognize my dependence on Him. It is not my power; it is not my love. My abilities are flesh. My abilities are works. They cannot produce spiritual results. I must, therefore, constantly rely on Him. I must ever remember that, "He is the vine and I am the branch." (John 15:5) The power, the life, and the love are in the vine. Without that life, the branch will be unproductive.

We are told in the New Testament to, "cease from our labors," and, "enter into His rest." I began to get an understanding, for really the first time in my Christian life what that really meant. I don't have to worry about being productive for God. I don't have to "try" to be loving. I don't have to try to "walk" the Christian walk. I don't have to "live for the Lord." All I have to do is trust. All of the labor to do everything right, say everything right, crucify my flesh, TRY – TRY – TRY, is just my flesh attempting to produce a spiritual result. And it never will happen! Only Jesus in me can produce a spiritual result.

I have begun to learn that my ability to trust the Lord in any area of my life is directly related to the revelation that I have of God's grace and His love for me. He will do for me, or in me, because He loves me. Thus, I can believe Him. I can trust Him. It's Jesus in me living this life.

CHAPTER FOURTEEN

HE LOVES "ME"

I am very grateful for the relationship, which my husband and I experienced. I have known so many people, both men and women, who have tried to find love, and feel that it has been just out of their grasp. The world is full, especially in this time in which we live, of people who have grown disenchanted about marriage and love between a man and woman. So many marriages end in divorce. People are afraid to get married, so they live together. Same sex couples are very common these days. Others are married, and stay married, but have just reconciled themselves to the fact that it simply is never going to be like they thought it would and they just go on, year after year, never having experienced the oneness they wanted. I certainly do not want to give the impression that I have all the answers or that we were a perfect couple. We had problems in our marriage, some of which I have already talked openly about on these pages. However, we were best friends for many years. Best friends, who worked together, played together, shared the same home, the same bed, the same family, and the same memories! Now, my best friend was gone!

For many years, when I was going through something which seemed difficult at the time, I would say to myself, "Now if others have gone through this and survived, I can too." I remember when I was in labor with my first child and the fear, pain, and trauma of childbirth seemed too much for me – young, inexperienced, and naïve as I was – I talked to myself in that manner. So, here I was, a widow, alone, in a new house, in a new city, and with more problems than I thought it was possible for anyone to have. Here I was, talking to myself! I told myself that I would not feel sorry for myself. As I began to take the initiative with myself and force my mind to "think" Word thoughts, instead of sulking and being depressed, the Lord began to minister to me from somewhere deep within me where He lives.

I resolved that I would not be morbid. I would not be depressed. I would not allow myself to become self-absorbed. I determined that I would allow myself to go ahead and grieve the loss of my husband. I happen to believe that it is an emotionally healthy thing to properly grieve. I did a lot of crying. I read old love letters we had written to each other. I cried some more. I cried over lost or incomplete dreams. I also decided that I would go ahead and talk about my husband as much as I wanted. We have always been a family who enjoyed laughing, teasing, and joking with each other. My husband was certainly a distinct personality so we had lots of funny things to remember. I allowed myself the luxury of remembering and talking about as many of these things as I could. I laughed with my daughter, my son, my sister and the rest of our family regarding every funny thing my husband had ever said or done that I could remember. You know what – it's therapeutic to do that! I believe that the Lord led me in that direction.

Through that time, the Lord began to minister to me about His love for me. All the verses in the Word of God which have to do with how much God loves us began to come alive to me. I had always known that God loved me – but His love began to take on a whole new meaning for me. He began to share with me that I could be ALONE BUT NOT LONELY because He had said that He would never leave me. He told me that His love for me was so really amazing that He cared about every tiny detail of my life and wanted to share it all with me. He told me that all of His power was available to me. He actually told me that I could look at it as, "God's Watch-Out-For-Me Power," and "God's Never-Forsake-Me Power." He told me that He would ALWAYS LOVE ME, no matter what. The Lord ministered to me, during this time, that this kind of moment by moment intimate, loving relationship is what He desires with every believer on the face of the earth, but most do not believe that He really loves them that much.

Consider this! The God of the universe – the One who spoke into existence the heavens and the earth – the One who had taken on flesh and had suffered and died, taking the sin of the world for us – actually wanted to have a moment by moment relationship with me, because He loves me. I had always, I believe, held Him at arm's length because I had viewed His love based on conditional love. I knew, in my mind, that God's love was unconditional. I had learned that, years before, when I had been believing for my daughter to return to us and to the Lord. I remember telling her one time when we were having a conversation back then that there was nothing she could ever do which would cause me not to love her – that my love for her was just like God's love – unconditional. Yet, here I was, all these years later, feeling like a little baby in the things of God, trying to get into my consciousness that God loved me unconditionally.

Let me explain what I mean. I was having trouble believing that my performance, and my husband's performance, over the last several years would not have an effect on God and his leading and treatment of me. As I prayed about my future, my mind replayed scene after scene, as distinct as a full-length movie, of our recent past. Everything that we had said and done, which had not been consistent with God's will and His call on both our lives, crowded my mind in living color. There were bad times in which I was consumed with guilt. I would remember the strong anointing which had been on my husband's life, especially when he had prayed for the sick, and the awful guilt I would feel for not having prayed him back to that call was almost more than I could bear. I know now that my precious Lord Jesus was not responsible for this onslaught of mental anguish. It was not the Holy Spirit. The Holy Spirit has come to convict the world of sin, of righteousness, and judgement. I am not of this world. I am in the world but not of the world. The Holy Spirit has not come to give me a guilty conscious. He has come to rid me of sin-consciousness. He has come to teach me that I am the righteousness of God in Christ.

I began reading the New Testament in the light of God's love for me. I began to pray and ask Him to reveal His love to me. Could it really be true, that He would allow me to pick up where I left off with Him, just as though I had never messed up? I think, somewhere, in the recesses of my mind, that I believed something like this. "Yes, God would certainly forgive me for messing up. Yes, He would consider it all a thing of the past; but I had made some messes and I was going to have to clean them up myself. I couldn't expect God to clean up messes for me when I had so let Him down. I couldn't expect God to still want to use me in the ministry after me fouling up so badly." I think so differently now that it's hard for me to write these words, realizing that it was exactly the way I was feeling a little while back. As I read the Word, in the light of His love for me, I began to have my thinking changed!

His love for me does not depend on my performance. His love is not conditional. He doesn't love me IF I do everything right; IF I don't foul up; IF I hurry up and confess my sin; IF I don't make too many messes!

He loves me – with no conditions to it. He loves me, plain and simple. There is nothing that I can ever do that can make Him not love me.

This is what I discovered as I pondered His love. If I believe that God's love for me is dependent on my performance, I will never believe that He will do the things for me that it says in His Word that He will do. Jesus made some pretty fancy promises as to what a believer could expect from Him and the Father, through the Holy Spirit. In order for me to believe those promises with all my heart, which is what faith is, I must believe that He will do them for me because He loves me. Period! It absolutely is not, and cannot be, dependent on my performance. My performance had absolutely nothing to do with me getting saved in the first place, and it has absolutely nothing to do with God's love for me, now that I am His child. In Galatians 5:6, it says, "……..but faith working through love." (NASB) I had always understood that verse to mean that in order for me to use faith, I had to operate in love. I now saw it in a whole new light. I could not ever be effective in using faith unless I could truly receive His love for me. His love for me is the basis of faith in my life. How can I pray for anyone, or anything, and really believe that He will do it because I ask Him to, if I do not believe with all my heart that His love for me is unconditional? I cannot!

I began to thank Him for His love for me. I praised Him for His love – not that I love Him but that He first loved me. His love for me took on new life – new meaning. His love for me became bigger than my failures. The more I concentrated on His love for me, the less I concentrated on my performance. I began to understand how Peter could "get over," his betrayal of Jesus and preach the first sermon of the church. He concentrated on how big and wide the love of God is! You cannot concentrate on your own failures, your own performance, your own sin, or your own guilt! You must move away from that into His love.

Performance-oriented Christianity is all most of us have ever known. Most of the church – liturgical, fundamental, denominational, non-denominational – has based its view of the Christian life on the way the world thinks or what religion says rather than what the Bible says. In the world, performance is everything. If you perform badly, you pay – one way or the other. By the same token, religion – even the religion of the Old Testament – requires good performance or payment. However, my friend, when we come to Jesus, accepting what He has done on the cross as personally for us individually, our payment has been made. God the Father accepted the payment of the blood of Jesus, the Son, on my behalf. The payment has been made! When I came to Jesus, His blood did not just pay for everything up to my acceptance of it and then I was on my own. If God required me to pay for my bad performance after I am saved, or to atone in some way, or suffer a little bit, I believe that it would be an insult to the blood of Jesus. I cannot add anything to what Jesus did on the cross. His payment was perfect. Whether it's penance in liturgical Christianity, or wailing over sin at the altar – with repentance until you look and feel really guilty – in fundamental Christianity, God's love and acceptance of us, and His willingness to help us, is not affected. It's us who are affected. We somehow feel better. We feel like we have paid. Wasn't the blood of Jesus good enough? Did we have to add to it? No! A thousand times No!

Please understand that I am speaking about the relationship between God and us. I am not speaking right now about our relationships with other people. If we have wronged society in some way, society may require us to pay. However, while we pay society for that in which we have offended society, we may be assured of the love of God. If, through our wrong actions, we have messed up other lives, love compels us to do what we can to make things right. But, "making things right," never gives us the right to mess up other lives again. I have known women and men who, through ignorance and sin, had divorced their mates and married others, and then wanted to discard the present mate to marry the first one again. Two wrongs do not make a right. We must receive God's love where we are in our lives and let Him orchestrate things for us. We cannot orchestrate things for ourselves. That gets us into trouble.

However, I had my own life to live by myself now. I did not have others for which I was responsible. It was only me! Therefore, in the strictest sense, I only had me to consider. Just the Lord and me!

Does the knowledge of God's love and forgiveness give us a license to just go do anything we want, anytime we want because we know that God won't be mad at us? The Apostle Paul dealt with that issue in the book of Romans. Please don't think that I am saying that we should just go wild with our lives. That is definitely not what I am saying. The more I comprehend the love of God – its length, depth, width, and breadth – the more I want to walk intimately with Him every moment of every day. When I miss it, when I foul up, I want to run to Him quickly and bask in His love for me. I want to tell Him that I'm so grateful that I am forgiven.

As I meditated more on God and His love and less on me and my performance, I began to realize that God had never given up on me. He had told me in Rom. 11:29, "For the gifts and the calling of God are irrevocable." (NASB) He had not taken His gifts back; He had not revoked His call. He would help me with the problems that I had and He would show me the way out. He loved me! He loved me! He loved me! It became a song in my heart, which was bigger than any failure. He would lead me. All I really had to do was trust that love. It might look as though nothing had changed, that my problems were still huge, that my life was still the same. But – He loved me! All I had to do was trust!

Was it too good to be true? Most of the church world would say that it was. Most ministers would avoid talking about it if they could because they just didn't know what to say. The general consensus is that people just lose their usefulness to God if they let too much time go by. They would never say that God wouldn't forgive you, but they would be hesitant to say that God would restore – that, in fact, the Lord would allow you to just pick back up where you left off. Making you pay a little, suffer a little, wait a little – that's natural, human, mental reasoning. That's conditional love – love with conditions attached. If you do this; if you do that; if you perform well; if you do it right, say it right; prove that you can really be trusted now – then you may be loved. God's love is unconditional. There are no conditions attached.

He just loves you and His promises are just as much for you now as they ever were!

I began to realize that we can change – God does not. We may mess things up – God straightens them out. We confuse the issues – His plan never changes. We think that we have fouled up so bad that God can never get it fixed so that we can be used by Him again – He still has a plan and a purpose – a destiny – and the ability and power to put it all in place. All it takes is believing Him. All it takes is yielding to Him. All it takes is trusting Him.

God could and would work it all out. He was willing to work it out. He loved me. He really, really loved me!

CHAPTER 15

WHO AM I, REALLY?

I have said, previously, that these things which I am sharing with you are discoveries which I have made about God and about me. Some of these discoveries were happening to me simultaneously; however, I feel like it is beneficial for me to go into them individually, rather than just lump them all together. It is easier for us to understand. Therefore, what I am going to say now was going on in me as I was dealing with the other discoveries, which I have already mentioned.

I have said, previously, that I had told the Lord that I wanted my life to count for something for eternity. I had told Him that I wanted to know that I was exactly where I was supposed to be, doing exactly what I was supposed to be doing for the rest of my life. I had also told the Lord that I didn't want to play games ever again in my life. I wanted to be transparent. What I was on the inside I wanted to be on the outside. However, in order for that to be the case, you have to know who you are. I had been a wife; I had been a mother; I had been a pastor's wife; I had been a teacher; I had been the administrator of our church; I had held lots of job titles along the way of my life. But who was I? I have made it quite clear on these pages that my life revolved around my husband. I have made it clear that my husband and my marriage had first place in my life instead of Jesus having first place in my life. I believe, with all my heart, that this is the case with many, many people in the Body of

Christ today. Other people, and other situations, have become the focus of the life, rather than Jesus, and it is the primary reason that we have not accomplished in our own little part of the world what we would like to for the Lord. We can never achieve the spiritual results we all would like to have in our lives until we make this correction. He absolutely must be first!

It would be very difficult to try to name all the ways in which people put others first, rather than Jesus, but the most common of these are the ones who are closest to the heart. It is clear from the Word of God that we are to take very seriously our roles in life such as wife, husband, child, parent, brother, sister and other close relationships; however, those roles should never become more important to us than the Lord.

There are several portions of Scripture, which have been hard to understand for most of us, and we have, therefore, skipped over them. Preachers and teachers have often given explanations, which hold to the letter of the law, and they have been harsh. I am referring to places like Mat. 8:21 where a disciple asked Jesus for permission to go and bury his father and Jesus, seemingly harsh, told him, "Follow Me; and allow the dead to bury their own dead." (NASB) Another place is Luke 8:21. Jesus' mother and brothers had come to where He was and couldn't get to Him. He was told that they wanted to see Him. But He answered and said to them, "My mother and My brothers are these who hear the word of God and do it." (NASB) I believe that the Lord has a spiritual principle for us in these portions of Scripture and others like them. It is this! Absolutely no one should be more important to us than Jesus! Absolutely no one is more important to Jesus than us, individually. What a truth! This is fundamental to experiencing in our lives what I believe God wants for each of us to experience. I do not believe that Jesus was saying to take lightly the relationships in our lives. That is contrary to other teaching of His. I believe He was saying that He absolutely must be first in our lives.

What I believe has happened in the Church is this. People come to Jesus – they get saved! They are excited and they expect for the Lord to now control everything and make everything different. They do not really understand very much about spiritual things and when things do not change as they had assumed they would, they pretty much go back to living their lives like the rest of the world lives. They do not know how to appropriate the life of grace for themselves. The Church is full of people whose lives are identical to people who have never been born again. I'm not talking about what they do for entertainment, what they eat or drink, where they go, etc. In other words, I'm not thinking here of the normal "do's and don'ts" which have been so much a part of legalistic thinking and connected with Christianity. I am talking about the very essence of the life of a Christian. The believer is, yes, on his or her way to heaven. But that is just the end result. The life lived is to be a moment by moment experience with the Son of God who has come to live in that believer. The life, therefore, though still in the world, should be as different from the world as Jesus' life was from the world. That kind of thinking may sound extreme to you but I believe it is the thinking, which flowed freely through the early Church. After those early Christians had come to Jesus, they didn't look at their lives the same way as they did before. They didn't think the same. They had a different agenda concerning everything in life. His name was Jesus. Everything and everybody now had to be second to the wonderful Lord who had been raised from the dead and who had taken sin, Himself, and given eternal life. That makes you think different. You don't approach your mate, your children, or anyone you love the way you did before. You don't approach what you do every day – work, study, etc. – in the same way you did before. You don't even think about your body as you did before. Your body has become a temple for Him. I'm not talking about rules and regulations now; I'm talking about freedom. I'm talking about adoration. It's freedom because you are no longer a slave to whatever you had been before. It's adoration because you love Him so much.

Our precious mates – the ones we have chosen to share our lives with – must come second to the Lord. Our children, as much as we love them, cannot consume us and be more important to us than the Lord. Our grandchildren, our parents, our other relatives all must come after the Lord in importance in our hearts.

In today's world, there are many other things, which vie for first place in our lives. To many people in full-time ministry, their ministries have become first in their lives – first before even the Lord. Their ministries consume them. To many others, their jobs are on those thrones in their hearts. The job has become the all-consuming thing in life. To the person in that position, that is not an easy thing to see. The job is so important. The ability to support the family comes from that source. The ability to give into the Gospel comes from that source. It is hard to separate the "what has to be," from the "what does not have to be." Very often, what a person does for a living becomes who he or she is. That becomes their identity. You are not your job! You are a unique individual who is very important to Jesus. Whatever title you hold, no matter how important it is, is not who you are. I have discovered that the attitude of the heart is much more important to Jesus than anything else. A person who comes to Him, honestly, and tells Him that things have gotten out of line, and he or she doesn't know how to change it, and asks for His help, will always receive it. Honesty before the Lord is very important. Why do we think we can "pull the wool over His eyes?" There is always the chance that one might have to actually tell the Lord, "I know I really ought to want to put you first, ahead of ......, but the truth is, I don't want to. However, I am willing for you to give me that desire in my heart. I believe that you can give me the desire to put You first. Please do that."

I am convinced that there are people in the Body of Christ who need to be healed, and who believe in divine healing, and yet will never be physically healed. The reason they will not is because they and their illness, or physical infirmity, have become one. They are one with their sickness in their own eyes. They cannot fathom not having their physical problem. Their lives are consumed, not with Jesus, but with their problem. Please do not misunderstand what I am saying to mean that I do not have compassion for the sick. I certainly do and I pray for the sick all the time. I have not always walked in 100% of the divine health that I desire to walk in and I am endeavoring to walk in it more each day. That is my desire. I'm not there yet. I am grateful for doctors and medicine and have partaken of my share of both. However, I still believe that, sometimes, with some people, physical problems, or even emotional problems, have become so much the central part of lives, that there is such a comfort level with the problem, that it makes it almost impossible to imagine not having it. It is the focus around which that person lives. "It" is on the throne of the heart.

There are any number of things in life – from people, whom we love dearly, to keeping these "temples" fit - which can become first in our lives. Jesus must be first in our lives. All of these other things, as well as our loved ones, are important. But not more important than Jesus!

I began to see that I really didn't know who I was. I had been my husband's wife for so long that my own individual and unique identity had been hidden. I hadn't intended for it to be that way. My husband certainly never intended that to be the case. He was always very proud of any accomplishment of mine and was always generous with praise. However, my own insecurities, as a person, which had been with me all my life, had propelled me to submerge myself as an appendage to my husband. I saw myself as an extension of him, rather than unique in my own personality.

Jesus is the One, who can show us who we really are, and how unique and precious we individually are to Him. I know of no other way that better explains how unique each of us is to the Lord, than the natural relationship of a parent to each of his or her children. No one child can take the place of another. Each child is unique and special to the parent. As the mother of two children, I am very much aware that each child holds a special place in my heart. How much more is that possible with our Heavenly Father! Why should we be surprised that the God of the universe is able to experience that with us, His children? Every single one of us is important. We all have a place in His family.

There are many people, I believe, who go through their lives with a wrong mental attitude, which is a humanistic approach to what I am talking about spiritually. Some start out in life as being very selfish children and just grow up to be self-centered adults. Others, perhaps, have felt inferior and, through input from some source, they have decided that they have rights and must assert themselves and what they want. The way they got to be the way they are is not nearly as important as seeing that the attitude is a self-centered one and can never lead to a spiritual result and true happiness. The humanistic approach is, "I am somebody. I am important. I have rights. I have a right to have things my way." The spiritual attitude, which I am talking about is, "I am special and unique to my Heavenly Father and He loves me so much that He is vitally interested in everything in my life. He will see to my happiness. He will take care of everything for me. I do not need to see to it all myself. I am a servant to my fellowman because Jesus lives in me and that's what He does."

I began to see myself in my true identity. I am a unique human being on this planet, all by myself. I am a born-again child of God because I have accepted Jesus Christ into my life. My Heavenly Father has adopted me into His family and the Holy Spirit has come to live in me on this planet. He has come to help me, comfort me, guide me, and teach me in every area of my life. Whatever I need in my life, He has promised to give me. He has made many, many promises to me. All I have to do is believe them.

I saw that I didn't have to plan my course. All I had to do was believe. I saw that my one main thing to do was worship Him. I remembered what Jesus had said to Martha when she was complaining about Mary not helping her with the work but, instead, sitting at Jesus' feet. He said that (my interpretation) Mary had chosen the most important thing. I began to see that, as I worshipped Him, He would lead me where He wanted me to go. I need not be frustrated and anxious about it. Many in the Body of Christ are frustrated about what they are supposed to do for the Lord. They are supposed to worship Him. I can hear them saying, "Yes, Lord, I will worship You, but what do you want me to do?" The answer again is to WORSHIP HIM. Take Him at His word and believe Him. Worship Him.

CHAPTER SIXTEEN

FINDING MY NICHE

For many, many years I have known the value of being a part of a local body of believers. Before my husband and I went into the ministry ourselves, we were in local churches. After we began pastoring, of course, the local church was the focus of our ministry and we believed intently on its importance.

At this new point in my life, I wanted desperately to be a part of a local church. I just couldn't seem to find where I fit. I was living in a new area, after my husband's move to heaven, and I visited many churches in the area. They were all lovely people and I tried my best to fit in. It was difficult, at first, to go places, like church, by myself, but I knew I had to, so I did.

I have believed for a long time that each person has a personal destiny. Then, when a person is born again, that person has a function in the Body of Christ to enter into the Great Commission by telling people about Jesus and helping to make disciples of all men. However, we are all different and the way we fit into that purpose and plan is unique for each one of us. In every church which I would visit in the new area to which I had moved, I would try to see myself as a part of that body but, somehow, something was not right. I don't mean there was anything wrong with them. Neither was there anything wrong with me. We just weren't connecting – and I knew it!

At the same time that I was becoming a worshipper and endeavoring to find my way, I began to have a desire to make contact with some friends of mine from previous years who were pastors in my hometown area. My husband and I had known this pastor and his wife for many years and, at one point, had been very close to them. I had absolutely no way of knowing this, but they had been going through much the same type of spiritual awareness that I had been going through. They had become dry and bored with hum-drum, charismatic Christianity and had sought the Lord for newness – for freshness – for awareness of Him. He had been answering those prayers by teaching them about individual intimacy with the Lord and by enlightening the eyes of their understanding to the message of, "GRACE." This is the message, which I have been writing about on these pages – this message of grace. This message says that you live the Christian life the same way you got saved – by grace; that God loves you unconditionally and there is nothing you can ever do to cause Him not to love you – because of His grace; that God is a good God and that He will never do anything to hurt you – that He has given His most precious Son for you – because of His grace; that He has adopted you into His family and that you have been forgiven of your sins – past, present, and future – because of His grace; that, as His children, we do not have to run from Him if we miss it, and worry about Him being angry at us – that the punishment for sin was taken by Jesus – and that we can bask in His love for us, no matter what – because of His grace; that we no longer need to be performance-oriented but, instead, we can be Jesus-in-us oriented – because of His grace.

As I said, my pastor friends had been going through personal awakening and had come to the conclusion that the message of God's wonderful love and grace was the message to be preached by them. Much of what they had been learning and understanding from the Lord is what I had also been experiencing. I had not called it, "the message of grace;" I thought I was just finally, after all these years, getting it "right" with Jesus.

There were a series of events, which significantly changed the course of my life – from where I was to where He wanted me to be. The desire to communicate with these friends grew stronger. I didn't know if they knew that my husband had moved to heaven or not. I knew it would take me a good while to put together the letter that I wanted to write to them. During the time in which I was writing the letter, one Sunday morning, early, the Lord spoke to my son, who lived in the same general vicinity as my pastor friends, and told him distinctly to go to their church. The Lord called the pastor by name to my son. He obeyed the Lord and took his family to that church. There was a loving reunion and discussion between this pastor and my son about me, and the loss of my husband.

My son relayed all this to me by phone and I was amazed. I went ahead and finished the letter. They received my letter and communicated back to me. My mother was in a prolonged illness and we knew her passing was imminent. I had to travel to be with my mother – in my hometown, where my son and his family lived and where my pastor friends' church was. I ended up being there for several weeks. On my first Sunday in the area, I went to my pastor friends' church with my son and his family, and my sister and her family and, for the first time since my husband had been gone, I felt "at home." I felt safe in this group of people. I felt loved. I felt like I was among family and yet some of them I had never seen before. That's the way church is supposed to be – a loving, safe family. God's plan for the local church is for a group of people who are a part of the Body of Christ to be together in unity – in one accord – "on earth as it is in heaven." They are to be loving and accepting of one another. "By this shall all men know that ye are My disciples, if you have love one to another." (John 13:35)

I was very comfortable with these people and, over the next few weeks, I wished so badly for a church like this one close to my home. My mother moved to heaven exactly six months to the day after my husband. I figured they had quite a reunion. After all the funeral things which we had to do, it came time for me to go back to where my home was. As I look back on it now, it seems strange that I couldn't see it – that it was the Lord's will for me to be there with them in that church. However, I honestly couldn't see it. My daughter, son-in-law, and grandson were in that area where I lived and I couldn't bear the thought of leaving them. My son and his wife and four children were back in the hometown area, and the thought of being close to them was wonderful, but, as I said earlier, one child cannot take the place of another. In my mind, I just didn't really consider moving. Although my daughter only lived about ten minutes from me, often we would communicate by email, especially concerning emotional things. We discovered during this time of our lives that we could write easier than we could talk about deeply personal or highly emotional things. My daughter wrote me a very emotional and unselfish letter, in which she shared her heart with me and told me that she thought that moving back was what I was supposed to do. She said many, many beautiful, and personal, things, and, as I wept through that letter, I knew it was the will of God.

It was not an easy move to make. In some ways, I felt like I was leaving behind the last few years with my husband. Yet, at the same time, the lovely area, which had once been so romantic and beautiful to me, held me no more. I had my memories. I will always have them.

It didn't take me long. Once I knew what I was going to do, with my daughter's help, I moved. I came back to where I started. My hometown! Where I had been on the radio, and where the church had been! Was I afraid? No, I can honestly say that I was not. Deep in the center of my being, in that place where Jesus lives, I knew! I had peace! My friend, you can be in circumstances which are a bit scary, and in which you do not know what the next hour holds, let alone the next day, and still have "the peace of God, which surpasses all comprehension." (Phil. 4:7 NASB)

That first Sunday, it was like "party-time!" among us all, His kids. We had a time of rejoicing. It was as though everybody knew that was what I was going to do and I was the last one to know. Most of them were not surprised. They all seemed to know. Some had been praying in that regard. It just felt right! The will of God feels right. Others may look at it and think you have lost your mind but if you know that you know that you are in the will of God and that He is leading you, it feels right. Peace in my heart is the greatest way that I have ever found to know the will of God.

I immediately became a part of this church, but I had made a commitment to the Lord that I would not go looking for a place to minister. I looked at it this way. If God wanted me to minister in any way for Him again, then He was perfectly capable of opening up the way before me to bring it to pass. I just so enjoyed being with these brothers and sisters and being a part of what God was doing there.

I began to ponder His plan, His destiny, His "niche" for me, since I had made this move and I have come to discover some very important things in this regard. <u>You have to see yourself in His plan for you – with just you and Him</u>. To often in my life, I thought of His plan for me as involving others to cause it to come about. I saw people as hindering me or helping me to fulfill my destiny. I have discovered that if I think that I need the others close to me to walk in my destiny, then when they fail me, or fall short in any way, I think of them as hindering me also. As I had begun to find out as I had become a worshipper, it was all about just Him and me.

I have thought, "What would I do if through some strange turn of events, I was stranded on a deserted island all myself? What would I do if I were stranded all alone in a mass of humanity where no one spoke my language and I was all alone?" I would pray! I would seek Him! I would stand on His promises in His Word and trust Him to deliver me! I would have no one else to trust – and therefore no one else could hinder me. I began to think of this whole idea of *MY DESTINY* in the same way. If this was between me and God, then all I really needed to do was put my entire confidence in Him to cause it to unfold in my life and just do each day what I have been given to do.

All my life, I had allowed my own thinking about the influence of other people to help me or hinder me to keep me from walking in the things that I really wanted to do. Then, when they failed me, I blamed them. Internally, of course! Being the type of person I have always been, I would never have told them that face to face. However, the internal monologue on the inside of me – the way I thought, day in and day out, all my life – had kept me in bondage. "For as he thinketh in his heart, so *is* he." (Prov. 23:7)

I began to realize that the way I saw myself on the inside, in my heart, as being helped or hindered by those close to me had put me in a position of dependence on others rather than the Lord. I have pondered much on that verse from Col 2:10, "But ye are complete in Him." Does that really mean that no matter where I am, that He makes me complete? Does that really mean that He will help me, no matter what goes on around me? Could that really mean that He – by His power, His wisdom, His knowledge – can make everything work out for me to fulfill His plan for me, even if others seem to not be doing what I thought they would or should do? Does it mean that it's really never too late for me to walk in His destiny?

I had to honestly consider these questions and come to the conclusion that Jesus in me – whether anyone ever did what they were supposed to do with me – was enough! I have strong desires to write and teach His Word. I believe those desires came from the Lord. They are my passions. I have allowed my own thinking about the influence of others to keep me from fulfilling those things in my life. NO MORE!

The Lord has spoken to me many times since I have moved back to the area from whence I came. He has given me personal direction, in my heart, and He has spoken to me through prophetic utterance, using several of His people to do so. The Lord has confirmed, through others, what He has told me in my own heart. There are some things He wants me to do for Him and, bit by bit, He has begun to fill in more of the picture for me. He is so faithful. He is so good.

After I had been in the congregation for several months, my pastor asked me to begin to teach on prayer in the church. During one of these late Sunday afternoon teachings, the Lord spoke to him and told him to ordain me. I had been ordained many years before but this was a new time and a new place for me and I welcomed this "fresh" ordination, which really is a recognition by other ministers that the call of God is on a person's life. We had that service about two weeks later and that was a great day for me.

I teach frequently and my desire is to help people begin to live the lives that God purposed for them all along. I want them to find their purpose for living.

You see, I have established some absolutes in my life and these absolutes govern everything I teach and write. They govern the way I pray and the way I look at life in general.

- The first absolute is: <u>God is a good God and He loves us unconditionally</u>. There is nothing that we can ever do to make God not love us. He is our Father. He has translated us out of the kingdom of darkness and into the kingdom of light (His kingdom) and adopted us into His family. He is not responsible for bad things in our lives. He has no "bad" in Him. He is "Love."

- The second absolute is: <u>Salvation by grace through faith is a truth for the entire Christian life</u>. When a person comes to Christ, his sins – past, present, and future – are forgiven. Performance is not an issue. We receive from Him based on His love and goodness. Intimacy with Jesus is vital to walking in the spirit in the Christian life.

I am teaching everything that I teach in the light of God's grace. What do I mean? When I read, study, preach, or teach the Word, I do it in the light of grace. The epistles of the New Testament show the "revelation" of the "church," or the "mystery," as Paul called it. Sure, I preach the Old Testament, for its principles, types, and shadows but not for its rules. It is clear, from the writers of the New Testament, that legalism (religion) is the enemy of grace. You might think that would just make everybody go crazy – to not have rules! That's what they were afraid of in Paul's day too, and he addressed that on more than one occasion. But you see, friend, we do have one rule – it is the rule of LOVE. It is the same one that Jesus talked about. I have found that basking in God's grace causes me to fall more and more in love with Jesus. When you fall more in love with Jesus, when you spend time worshipping Him, both privately and corporately, all you want to do is walk closer to Him. Walking close to Jesus doesn't make you <u>want</u> to sin – it makes you <u>want not to</u>.

I have a heart to see the lost saved; however, it doesn't stop there. I want to see people who have been bound by the chains of legalism to be set free. I want people, who have been on the merry-go-round of trying to "perform" to get their prayers answered, to understand how much God loves them. I want to see families fall back in love with each other again as they understand that they can't ever make their flesh be spiritual – that it's Jesus in us who walks this Christian life. What freedom!

I want to see people healed, and pain and suffering gone, as people comprehend that God loves them enough to heal them. They can't earn it. They can't do it right, say it right, etc. In other words, it's not about their performance.

I am praying for people to see that it's not about us and how we perform – in other words, what we do or don't do! It's all about Him. He's already done it all. We can't add to what He has done. We must receive it by grace through faith. The church has sung songs for years and years about Jesus doing it all – but they didn't believe it. They tried to do it too. They thought they had to be a certain way, say a certain thing, follow a certain rule, repent enough, and on and on and on. All the time, He had already done it all.

I don't spend time in prayer begging God to forgive me of my sins. He already has. I don't beg Him to meet my needs. He has already said in His Word that He has. I thank Him for meeting my needs. I don't spend time in prayer begging for Him to make me holy. He said, in His Word, that He'd already done it. What I do in prayer is VISIT WITH HIM. Yes, I said, "visit!" God created man because He wanted a family. I see, as I read that story in the first part of Genesis, that God came to the garden in the cool of the day and I believe that He came to visit with the man and woman. I believe that fellowship or "visiting" should be a huge part of our prayer lives. Most Christians have grown so accustomed to asking, begging, quoting verses, etc., that they have forgotten to visit with Him.

I come from a family that has a long history of visiting with one another. Sunday afternoons were always a time to gather together and just visit. That is not just one person doing all the talking. If that takes place in a close family, someone will be sure to interrupt (lovingly) and everyone will be able to enter in again. Visiting is everybody talking – a little here and a little there. It is everyone else listening and paying attention to what is being said. It is caring.

I personally think that we have lost the art of visiting in our culture because we are all so busy in our lives and we have become accustomed to being entertained by television, movies, and computers. Thus, we don't know how to visit with God! Visiting with God is talking with Him and telling Him about everything – and listening to Him. It's being quiet sometimes. If you are asking Him for wisdom in certain situations, how can you hear what He has to say if you are always talking?

So, my friend, *MY NICHE* in life is sharing these things that I have learned with others – by teaching and writing. I have found my niche! Now, I don't mean to imply that I am walking in it to the degree that I want to. In fact, in some areas, I feel like I have just begun. But, you know what? It is the most exciting life on the planet! This life of being in constant communication with the creator of the universe and *KNOWING* that you are walking with Him, walking in Him, fulfilling the destiny, the plan, that He has for you. I love the way Eph 2:10 is translated in the Amplified Bible. "For we are God's [own] handiwork (His workmanship), recreated in Christ Jesus, [born anew] that we may do those good works which God predestined (planned beforehand) for us [taking paths which He prepared ahead of time], that we should walk in them [living the good life which He prearranged and made ready for us to live]." I had always thought that God's will, or His plan, or His destiny, or His niche was something very hard to find and that it was this narrow little path that was difficult and probably something that I didn't want to do. I have found the very opposite to be the case.

His niche for me fits me! After all, He designed it for me "ahead of time," knowing me intimately. He wants me to walk in it even more than I want to. He is not trying to hide it from me. He is not making it hard. He wants to show it to me. He planned it for me.

I have discovered that the niche for me in this life here on this planet is a melding together of my unique personality with His personality in me. I am not an afterthought – I am not an add-on – I am not somebody else's something! I am a very unique individual living here on this planet, in this time and place, by very planned design. I am His workmanship! There are things that He has planned for me to do, knowing that I would be living here and now – not 100 years ago nor 100 years in the future. I wasn't born in covered wagon days. I was born now. I was born in the United States of America to my parents in the 20th century. I was not a mistake. NEITHER WERE YOU! My role in life requires my very own distinct personality with His very own distinct personality in me to carry it out. I have certain personality traits and abilities which make me uniquely me and there are things I am designed to do. However, it takes Him in me and my reliance on

Him for those things to be perfectly fulfilled.

There have been millions (or trillions) of people on this planet – all unique in themselves – some of which have been very successful because of their abilities and traits. Think of what they could have accomplished for God on this earth had they allowed Him to work through them.

I want to allow Him to work through me. "For it is God which worketh in you both to will and to do of his good pleasure." (Phil 2:13) I have things I want to do and I enjoy doing but if I just try to do them in my own strength or ability, they will never accomplish what they could if there were done in His ability (grace). That way, I can never take the credit. It is Him in me. I have found my niche!

CHAPTER 17

THE SECRET OF JESUS LIVING

All of my life, and most especially since I have been a Christian and have studied the Word of God, I have believed that one should be able to live worry-free in this life. I could read in the Bible all the things that Jesus said and it seemed to me that He made it clear that one could live without strain, stress, and pressure. I constantly got the impression that life could be lived as He lived here on this earth. I didn't see Him "stressing out," worrying about money, health, loved ones, how things were going to work out, or the daily pressures of life. Loving people, no matter what they were like did not seem to be difficult for Him. However, for the life of me, all those years, I couldn't seem to figure out how to do that. Even more, I didn't know anybody who did know. I heard tapes by great preachers and I read books written by Christians but as far as ever actually knowing anyone personally who had learned the "secret of Jesus living," I never did. That is not to say that the people who wrote the books and preached on the tapes didn't know – I am just saying that somehow the message of "how to do it," never got through to me. There were methods of how to make things work. There were steps to pray. There were ways to perform. I had done it all. I had fasted to become more spiritual. I had prayed for hours and hours at a time. I had wept! Being a reader, I had read many, many books on prayer, on healing, on finances, on being spiritual, on growing a church, on family life, and on numerous subjects – always trying to find the key

– the "secret to Jesus living."

Walking in love all the time, even with the people that I cared deeply about was much too hard. I couldn't even begin to understand how to walk in love with people who were mean to me. However, Jesus walked in love with people who hated Him – and He said for us to be like Him. In fact, He commanded it.

I said, in a previous chapter, that every new experience that my husband and I grasped at was viewed as perhaps being the key for which we had been looking. The key to living this life! Nobody ever told us! I'm not blaming anybody – You can't give out what you do not have. However, because of all the reading I've done and all the listening I have done, I must assume that not many have had a grasp of the part that the love and grace of God play in living this life. There has been so much emphasis on performance. Doing it right! Saying it right! And all along, it was so simple!

When Jesus came into me in the person of the Holy Spirit, when I was born again, He brought everything into me that I need to live this life. (2 Peter 1:3) All through the Old Testament, He gave clues, through the prophets, that He was going to live in His people. When Jesus died on the cross, was buried, was resurrected, and ascended, He came (in the person of the Holy Spirit) to live in people who would receive Him. The New Testament is full of this teaching. All that He is, all that He has done, and all of His power has come to live on the inside of every believer! We have not believed that. We have talked about it; we have sung about it; we have read about it; but we have not believed it. The whole Christian life is a life of faith. We do not believe that God IS because we see Him with our physical eyes. We believe that God IS because, first of all, we want to. He has created man with the desire to know his creator. Then we believe that God IS because His Word has declared Him to us. Because His Word, when it was preached to us, awakened in us that desire to know Him, we believed. Therefore, that same Word that told us about what He had done, through Jesus, to open up the way for us to be reconciled to God, also declares to us what He has done in order for us to live this life. He has actually come to live in us to live this life for us. The only thing we have to do is believe it!

So what does all that mean? It means this! In my flesh – my

human-ness, my mental awareness, my ability, my education, my will (willpower), my skills, my genetic background, my race, my nationality or any other thing in my personality – no matter how good any of it is – I do not have the ability to live the Jesus life. I cannot live the Jesus life any more than I could have saved my soul from eternal damnation. It took the perfect Son of God, Jesus – the Son of Man – to take my sin upon Himself for me. He knew I could not live the way His Word directed me to without Him coming to actually live the life in me. To the degree I will trust Him to do so, He will do it! The trouble is – we haven't trusted Him to do it. We have tried to do it ourselves. Isn't that amazing! We couldn't save ourselves but we have thought we could live this life after we were saved. We found it so difficult to do, however; so we took rules and regulations from the Old Testament and made them to try to apply to our new lives. We took the suggestions that the apostle Paul and others gave to the churches of their day – and their culture – and have made them rules and regulations for our day and our culture. We have done the same thing that the Jewish Christians did and we have whole letters in our New Testament devoted to correcting them about it. And yet we didn't get it!

It is so very simple – yet we have made it so hard. It is me realizing that I cannot do it and yielding to Him and asking Him to do it. Jesus will never steamroll over us. He will never "make" someone get saved. It is His will that all men be saved (2 Peter 3:9) but millions of people have gone into eternity without knowing Jesus as their Savior. He does not "make" them get saved. Likewise, He will never steamroll in your life and "make" you do anything. He will not let His love be lived out through your life unless you recognize that you need Him to do it and yield to Him. His peace is in me. His love is in me. His hope – His strength – His power – His healing – His gifts (for all who have the need of them) – His wisdom – and on and on and on! Everything of God, in Jesus, is in me. All it takes is me realizing it and trusting Him. It does not take another experience. Praise God for the wonderful experiences I have in God. I am so grateful for all of them. But those experiences do not make it possible to live the Jesus life. Jesus in me makes it possible to live the Jesus life. Without Him I can do nothing.

So many today are trusting in the gifts of the Spirit to help them live the Jesus life. I so value the gifts of the Spirit. Prophecy has been a real blessing in my life and has given me hope and encouragement when I needed it. However, I cannot trust prophecy to help me live the Jesus life. With the baptism in the Holy Spirit, came tongues, or as I like to refer to it, my prayer language. There are so many wonderful benefits to tongues and I pray in tongues (commonly referred to as 'in the Spirit') every day – sometimes for long periods of time. I pray much for others when I don't know how else to pray. Sometimes I pray for myself when I don't know how else to pray. I pray for my family, my church, my pastor, my friends, etc. and sometimes I pray (I believe) led by the Holy Spirit, for people I don't even know. I am always built up when I pray in tongues. (Jude 20) However, I cannot trust tongues to live the Jesus life. Jesus in me is the power to live this life.

In other words, I am saying that no matter how wonderful the gifts of the Holy Spirit are, we cannot put all our hope, confidence, and trust in them to live this life. They are gifts – primarily to give of God to others. God is such a lover of mankind and has all kinds of ways in which He can bless mankind. The gifts of the Holy Spirit are for that purpose. They were never intended by God to be used by the church for private "Bless me" clubs.

So, my friend, the "secret to the Jesus life" is simply – Jesus in me – me realizing it and trusting Him to do it. It's me yielding to Him!

Thank You, Lord Jesus!

CHAPTER 18

THE JOURNEY FROM HERE TO THERE

One of the major things I have discovered about myself in this time of learning which I have been involved in is that I had never been content in just living in "today." I began to consider my attitudes and my internal monologue on a day to day basis and I found that I was always thinking about the next step, the next thing, the next place, etc. I had never given that too much consideration before. It seemed to me that if you had a plan and knew where you wanted to be, then all your energies, time, finances, thinking, and prayer should be directed toward that goal. The only problem is that when you think that way then you don't really enjoy where you are "right now." You are always living toward the future.

One of the powerful things I have noticed about the Apostle Paul, as I have read the Book of Acts and the Epistles which he wrote, is that no matter where he was, what was going on, or how bad or good things were, he had learned the secret to being content in his "today." As I have read and have thought about that, I have seen that come through in his writings and in the things which were written about him. Phil 4:11 says, "Not that I speak in respect of want: for I have learned, in whatsoever state I am, *therewith* to be content." 1 Tim 6:8 says, "And having food and raiment let us be *therewith* content."

What happens in your life when you are always consumed with the next moment, the next hour, the next day, the next year and so on is that you really never truly are content in your today. I thought back to the times when, even in my youth, I would plan a big evening – lots of fixing, and preparation! Then, when that evening would come, while I was in the very moments of the evening which I had planned, I would be thinking of the hours following, or the next day. When my children were young and my husband and I would have an occasional evening out by ourselves, while we were at dinner or in the movie, I would be distracted by thoughts of "later," or tomorrow. As I considered this, I discovered that I had never truly learned to be content in my moment called, "now."

When you live that way, it becomes such a way of life and such a habit pattern in your life that you don't really even know that you are doing it. It has become the only way you know how to live. I thought back to the times when I have had big events in my life and I see that this way of thinking prevents a person from ever truly enjoying the high moments of life. It also prevents you from accomplishing the marvelous things in "today," which you could accomplish because you are fixed on tomorrow. Then, when you get to tomorrow, it is never as satisfying as it could be because you are then fixed on the next day or the next thing.

The Bible has something to say about this. Earlier I have said that the Old Testament can give us help for living and it gives us types and shadows for our understanding of things. We, as born again believers, get our doctrine from the New Testament. However, if we will keep that in mind, we can learn from the things we read in the Old Testament. Deut. 28 is commonly known as the "blessing and cursing" chapter. It told the Old Covenant believers that if they would do certain things that God said, they could expect certain blessings. It also told them that if they would not do what God said, they could expect the curses. We know that Jesus took the curse of the law for us and we are in Him. We are heirs of God and joint-heirs with Christ. So I do not read this chapter in fear of the curses. But I can learn some things. In verses 65-67, which I am not going to quote here, it primarily says that one of the curses for not obeying God is never being satisfied in your today. (My interpretation.) In the morning, you wish it was evening and in the evening, you wish it was morning. That is certainly a lack of contentment or satisfaction.

So, as I thought about these things, I began to see that in living this Jesus life, it could be possible for me to have my dreams for tomorrow and all the things that I wanted to do – that I could actually plan and organize for tomorrow – and yet fully be content in the moment I was living and enjoy it to the hilt. My – My – My!! What a novel thought for me and what a change that would be.

Also involved in this thinking, is the frustration of an organizer. I suppose that people who just live each moment with not much planning and just seem to take things as they come would not understand the mind of an organizer. However, I have always been an organizer. I find life to be very confusing if I do not organize things so I know where things are, when I am to do this and that, where I am to be and when, and how I am to do things, etc. I make lists; I like to keep accurate records; I can pretty well always find things in my living space; I am seldom ever late with where I am supposed to be. More often than not, I am early. More times than I care to tell you about I have sat parked on the street, not going into someone's home yet, because I was early. I don't like to be late so I always plan on plenty of time. I am also a pretty good judge of time. I can usually assess how much time has gone by before I look at my watch. One thing that my husband and I were pretty well-matched on was that he was the same way about time. He was not always so organized with other things but we always planned our time well and never argued about one causing the other one to wait, as some couples do. This was never a problem to us. Thank the Lord!

However, along with this type of personality comes the planning in one's mind of how things are going to be when that moment arrives. Now, one of the big problems with this is that almost every "moment" involves other people. With this type of personality, one has the tendency to imagine the whole scenario ahead of time – what people will say, how they will act, what they will do. What huge problems that can cause because people seldom ever say or do what you think they are going to from the way you have imagined it. Therefore, in the midst of every situation, for which you have planned and organized, when people do not do or say as you have imagined that they would, you are disappointed and frustrated. Therefore, you are not only upset because it isn't the way you think it should be but you are also thinking about later, or tomorrow, or next month, or next year! You tend to never be really happy in the moment.

I thought about the Apostle Paul, a prisoner in Rome, thinking about all the things he wanted to still do, all the churches he wanted to visit, and yet – there he was – a prisoner. If ever there was a Christian who could have been frustrated with the way things were, it was him. Yet, he said, "I have learned, in whatsoever state I am, *therewith* to be content." This change in thinking is absolutely necessary not only to alleviate stress in one's life but also to be really useful in the things of God. As I have contemplated my future, my tendency is to just hurry up and get things moving so I can get to that place called, "There." I want to get from "Here," to "There." But it is a journey! I have found that one of the biggest struggles I have encountered is to learn how to plan and dream toward my destiny – that place called, "There" – and yet be content and happy in my moment called, "Here." I see where I want to be, where I want to go, what I want to do and in my flesh, that is where my mind tells me I will find contentment. However, that is not the Bible way. That is not the way of the Spirit of God. That is not the Jesus way.

What it boils down to is trust. Do I trust the Lord to bring me to that place that He saw me in before the foundation of the world? Eph. 1:4 in the Amplified Bible says, "Even as [in His love] He chose us [actually picked us out for Himself as His own] in Christ before the foundation of the world, that we should be holy (consecrated and set apart for Him) and blameless in His sight, *even* above reproach, before Him in love." I love the way Eph. 2:10 is stated in the Amplified Bible, "For we are God's [own] handiwork (His workmanship), recreated in Christ Jesus, [born anew] that we may do those good works which God predestined (planned beforehand) for us [taking paths which He prepared ahead of time], that we should walk in them [living the good life which He prearranged and made ready for us to live]." It just makes it so clear in this passage that He has a plan for me and if I will just do what He shows me to do for today, He has the power and the desire to bring me into that place. That place called, "There!"

You see, I have been so fearful in my life of messing things up so badly that I could never get "There." That very fear itself has the capacity to keep me in bondage and keep me struggling and frustrated. Not only was I afraid that I could mess things up but I was afraid that others could mess it up for me. For so long, I felt like others close to me could hinder me from walking in my destiny. What I have come to see is that the only one who can hinder me from walking in my destiny is me. What I believe about myself in my heart is what determines my life. How often have you heard, even in the secular world, that people have believed from the time they were children that they were going to do this or that. There are cases of children being in extremely bad situations and yet strongly believing that they were going to be successes and then they become just that.

Now – if I believe that others are hindering me, then I am hindered! It's what I believe in my heart. I am the one who controls what I believe in my heart. I am the only one who has the ability to persuade my heart. Others may say things or do things and it is my reaction to those things that makes me believe in my heart toward success or failure, prosperity or lack, healing or sickness, peace or frustration, and all the other things that face us in life. So – my believing that others could hinder me from walking in my destiny definitely hindered me. The others couldn't hinder me. My *believing* that they could hinder me is what hindered me. In my heart is where I believe – either good or bad. Nobody controls my heart but me.

Now – let me say one thing here that we need to consider in this realm. The Apostle Paul gives us a clear picture through his writings in the Pauline Epistles about this. He could see that there were people out to destroy him. They wanted to kill him in order to shut him up. Paul knew that if they accomplished that he would not be able to fulfill his call which was preaching the Gospel to the gentiles. When he asked the believers to pray that he would be delivered, which he did in several different places in his letters, I am convinced that it was not so that he could avoid suffering. He made it clear that he was ready to suffer for the Gospel, if necessary. However, he knew that there was a plan for him to reach many people in the then-known world for Jesus and if the unbelievers who were wanting to shut him up could accomplish that he would not be able to fulfill his destiny.

Therefore, it behooves us to not be ignorant of the "enemy's devices" and pray, operate in faith, and believe in our hearts to walk in those paths that He has for us.

I have, therefore, come to a place where I can trust Him in my heart to bring me to that place where I have been trying to get for so long. He can do it. He has the power to do it. He knows things I don't know. However, I do have a responsibility in this. My responsibility is to trust Him. The way I do that is by spending time with Him, fellowshipping with Him, which is really visiting with Him. When I visit with Him, I don't do all the talking. He shares with me. I don't hear an audible voice. He lives in me – in my spirit – and He gives me impressions and revelations from my spirit to my heart. He gives me understanding. He shows me what to do. He helps me. What I believe He is showing me from deep inside me where He lives will always be in agreement with His Word. He and His Word will always agree. If it appears that it does not, I pray and He will give me understanding.

With that kind of shift in my thinking, I can be content with where I am. If I know that I am doing what He has shown me to do for today, I can be satisfied today. Instead of being frustrated, I can be content.

CHAPTER 19

AND THE GRACE GOES ON.........

I have discovered so many wonderful things in the last few years and I am still learning more every day, about Him and about me. I am convinced that if we Christians truly believe what Jesus said when He, the Son of Man, walked on this earth, every single one of us would have a deep impact on our world. We have made it so hard because we didn't understand how easy He made it for us. Yes, it takes commitment or dedication; but that's what becoming a Christian is really all about – beginning to trust the Father for our lives. He did everything for us! He gave His Son. I like to call it "The Great Exchange." Jesus took our death and, in exchange, gave us life. He took our sin and gave us righteousness. He took our sickness and gave us health. He took our poverty and gave us prosperity.

Jesus said that His yoke was easy and His burden was light. He has been teaching me that all my struggling and working and frustration was because I was trying to carry the burden and pull the load – in my flesh. The grace for living came to each one of us the moment we were born again. When I think of all the things I TRIED to do for Him, all the ways I TRIED to witness, TRIED to make things work, TRIED to love.........Ah – all the time He was right there in me, willing to do it all for me. I didn't know! I knew He was there, but I didn't understand that it took me believing that

He would do it and turning it over to Him.

First of all, I had to just yield the right-of-way to Him. I used to sing the old hymn, "I Surrender All," but I didn't know how to do it. I wanted to surrender or yield and I thought I had (probably thousands of times, through the years) but I just didn't get it!

I want you to get it! My prayer is that you will. Your relationship with the Lord is unique and is between you and Him. I'm not going to give you steps for yielding. They never helped me when other people gave them to me in books. They just made me frustrated because I thought I had already done all of that.

I trust that you have been born again. If not, it's really not hard and it's not as spiritually complicated as some have made us to believe. It's just a matter of beginning to believe that God loves you and has provided a plan through the death, burial and resurrection of Jesus Christ for you to always be with Him, in His family. He's done all the work. All you have to do is believe it. You don't have to work for it. In fact, you can't! You can't try to make yourself better and you can't really do anything to deserve it or earn it. If you believe what I have been saying in this book about Him and you want to be in His family, just tell Him that. You don't have to say things a special way. Just tell Him what you feel down in your heart. Your heart is the center of your being. It's the place where you believe. Just tell Him that you believe in Him and want to be in His family and have Him in your life. The moment you, from your heart, express that to Him you are born again. He has come into your life and will never leave you or forsake you. You will never be alone again.

Now perhaps you are one, like I was, who has been born again and has dedicated and surrendered and yielded until you are worn out with trying to get it right with Jesus. Maybe you are one who has been seeking new experiences to try to find the key to living the Christian life. Then perhaps you are one who just never even thought about it much because you didn't know anyone who really took living the Christian life seriously – you just had your "ticket to Heaven," and that's all that really mattered. However, somehow this book ended up in your hands and you truly want to experience God as I have been talking about – you just didn't ever think it was possible. Or maybe you're the one who just got born again a few sentences back!

Well, whichever one you are, today is your day! I want you to find a time to be alone for a little while. I want you to sit quiet for a little bit without even trying to pray at first. I want you to think about what you have been reading and then about the Lord. Just sit and think about Him – His goodness, mercy, love, kindness, gentleness, generosity, and purity. Just think about the vastness of His love for you and what He went through so that you could be His child. What amazing love! My sister – my brother – His love truly is amazing. There is nothing like it in all the universe. And everything He's done, He's done for you. Don't try to be religious. Just begin to talk to Him from your heart. Tell Him how you feel.

As you do, I want you to just see yourself laying down all your effort, all your work, all your trying, all your worry and strain. I want you to tell Him that you are giving up all your "ways" and that you realize that He must do it because you can't. I tell Him that all the time about everything in my life. It's His grace that is sufficient for everything. I couldn't save myself. It took Him. I can't do the living. It takes Him. Tell Him that you give up trying to do it all. Ask Him to do the living through you. Tell Him that you're not even going to worry about it anymore. You're not going to try to figure it out. You're not going to be nervous or stressed. You're just going to trust Him and live from one moment to the next believing that He is taking care of everything. Decide to do the things that you have to do in your life trusting Him, moment by moment, to do what you can't do. In your flesh (your own ability), you cannot love the unlovely. Trust Him to do that. Your flesh doesn't have the wisdom to know what to do in certain circumstances. Trust Him for that wisdom. I say to Him all the time, "Lord, I don't know how to do this. Please show me what to do. I trust You." I say to Him, "Father, I trust You to watch out for me. You said You would never leave me or forsake me. I trust You to see to me."

That's the way I go through every day. Obviously, if I am around people, I must use some discretion about talking to the Lord. Think about the way Jesus acted around people and do what He did. (Of course, you'll have to read the Bible to see how He acted and what He did.) Jesus acted so normal around people that they called Him a friend of sinners, a glutton, and a winebibber. My goal is to go through life as a normal person, with a constant connection to the One who said that He would never leave me or forsake me.

Whatever you do, don't try to be religious. Don't try to put rules on yourself. Legalism (rules and regulations for behavior) is the enemy of grace. Jesus talked about that to the religious leaders of His day. Paul wrote about rules and regulations in almost every one of his letters to the churches. Just relax and, instead of concentrating on what you should or should not do, become conscious of the fact that He has come to live inside you. If you will trust Him, He will enable you and empower you to live this life – because He loves you.

You'll find that every day is new and exciting. He will cause you to see people differently than you have before. He wants you to see people the way He sees people – through His eyes of love. His Word will become more meaningful to you than it has ever been before. You will find it to be full of promises of what He said He would do for you. All you have to do to have them in your life is believe them. When you find a promise that He has made, tell Him that you believe it and that you trust Him for that in your life. You don't have to beg Him. He's already done it for you. You are His very special child – the child of His love.

Jesus and you,

And the grace goes on......

Jesus and me,

And the grace goes on......

We are family,

And the grace goes on......

CONCLUSION

On one of those occasions when I was worshipping the Lord, after my husband moved to heaven, He told me that He wanted me to write a book. I wrote it down that day. I have exactly what He said to me and the date on which He said it. This was very scary to me when He asked this of me because I had always been such a private person. I wasn't sure I had what it took to reveal so much of my life, both good and bad, in a way for all to see. I have always wanted to write, but I wasn't sure I wanted to write about so many personal details of my life.

The Lord talked to me that day and asked me if I really meant what I had said to Him. I told Him I did. He told me that if I really wanted to help people, I would be willing to let people see my wounds. He reminded me of when Jesus was with some of His disciples on the road to Emmaus. He went to their home and when He broke the bread and prayed, their eyes were opened, and they recognized Him. I personally believe that they saw where the wounds were in His hands. We know that His wounds were visible, because He told others to look at them. The Lord told me that, if I would be willing to let others see my wounds, which He had healed, they would be helped. He assured me that I didn't need to go into the gory details – it's a good thing, because I can't even remember some of them now anyway.

God has healed my wounds by His grace, through His faith. He will heal yours also.

Lovingly, in the name of Jesus,

Gloria Hartman

Printed in the United States
30293LVS00006B/286-339